Abraham
LINCOLN

Who will you get to know next?

Watch out for
Elon Musk and Emmeline Pankhurst

first names

Abraham
LINCOLN

Jonathan Weil

Illustrations by John Aggs

For Matilda

First Names: ABRAHAM LINCOLN
is a
DAVID FICKLING BOOK

First published in Great Britain in 2020 by
David Fickling Books,
31 Beaumont Street,
Oxford, OX1 2NP

Text © Jonathan Weil, 2020
Illustrations © John Aggs, 2020

978-1-78845-045-4

1 3 5 7 9 10 8 6 4 2

The right of Jonathan Weil and John Aggs to be identified
as the author and illustrator of this work has been asserted
in accordance with the Copyright, Designs and Patents Act 1988.

All rights reserved. No part of this publication may be reproduced,
stored in a retrieval system, or transmitted in any form or by
any means, electronic, mechanical, photocopying, recording
or otherwise, without the prior permission of the publishers.

Papers used by David Fickling Books are from well-managed
forests and other responsible sources.

DAVID FICKLING BOOKS Reg. No. 8340307

A CIP catalogue record for this book is available from the British Library.

Printed and bound in Great Britain by Clays Ltd, Elcógraf S.p.A

The facts in *First Names: Abraham Lincoln* have been carefully checked
and are accurate to the best of our knowledge, but if you spot something
you think may be incorrect please let us know.
Some of the passages in this book are actual quotes from Abe and other
important people. You'll be able to tell which ones they are by
the style of type: *Government of the people, by the people,
for the people, shall not perish from the Earth.*

CONTENTS

INTRODUCTION – HE'LL NEVER COME TO MUCH	7
1 – ABE MOVES HOUSE	10
2 – ABE'S ADVENTURES AFLOAT	20
3 – ABE STANDS AND FIGHTS	36
4 – LEGAL EAGLE ABE	49
5 – ABE GOES TO WASHINGTON	63
6 – ABE BOUNCES BACK	75
7 – ABE'S DARKEST HOUR	96
8 – ABE'S BIG SECRET	110
9 – ABE KEEPS HIS PROMISE	120
10 – ABE'S HAPPIEST DAY	134
TIMELINE	142
GLOSSARY	144
INDEX	146

Introduction – He'll Never Come To Much

12th February 1809 – Kentucky, USA

Nancy Lincoln gave birth to her second child in a rickety log cabin in the countryside. A few days later, her nine-year-old cousin Dennis came to visit. Nancy thought it would be pretty funny to see how Dennis dealt with a newborn baby, so she plonked her son into his arms and stood back to see what would happen.

> *Take him back. He'll never come to much.*

Nancy had to admit Dennis was probably right. Her husband, Thomas, was a carpenter and small-time farmer who **couldn't read or write**. Most likely, the baby would have an ordinary poor man's life. There was no reason to believe the world would ever know the name Abraham Lincoln.

The family lived in a log cabin, miles and miles from the nearest town, and although some say his mother taught him to read, Abraham **hardly ever went to school**. Then, when he was seven, the family were forced to move. Thomas was in trouble with the law:

he didn't have the right documents to prove he owned his farm, so he had to start all over again. They packed all their things onto a wagon, and set off on the long journey into the wilderness of Indiana . . .

Really? So you don't think they'll want to know you were a **champion wrestler**, travelled thousands of miles on a flatboat, gave the most **famous speech in history**, saved your country, **freed millions of people** from slavery . . . ?

You're too modest – more people have written books about you than about any other person . . . in history.

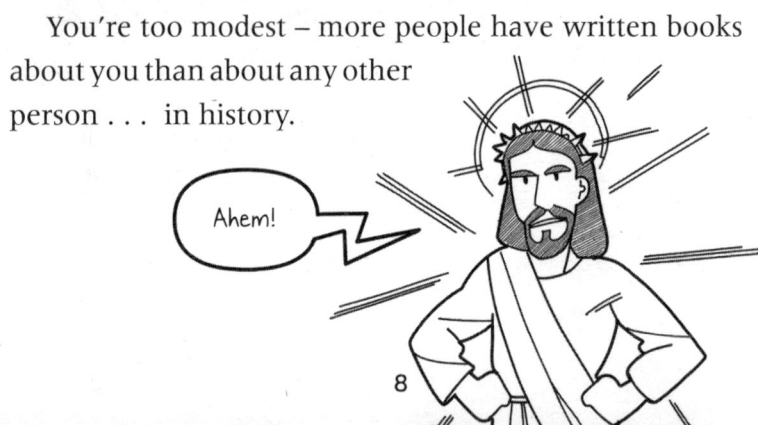

OK, apart from Jesus. But still – so many books that in 2010 the director of Ford's Theatre in Washington DC decided to build a tower out of them!

Well, there's **seven thousand** in this tower ... and that's less than half of them!

Message received. On with the story!

1 ABE MOVES HOUSE

Abe was seven years old in autumn 1816 when his family moved to Indiana. The land there was up for grabs – and once he'd claimed his new farm, Abe's pa wouldn't have to worry about those pesky legal disputes that had caused him to up sticks. It was the perfect place to start afresh. There was just the howling wilderness, **crawling with dangerous beasts**, to worry about – oh, and the fact they'd have no food, no house, no next-door neighbours . . .

Abe's family travelled light. They would build their own furniture when they arrived (just as soon as they'd finished building their house), so all they needed was an axe, tools, and the one thing they couldn't make themselves – his parents' feather mattress.

After days of hard travelling, the family crossed the Ohio River into the wild pinewoods of Indiana. From here they had to cut their own trail, hacking at undergrowth and chopping down trees. It was backbreaking work – but Abe was going to have to get used to that.

Abe was big for a seven-year-old – big enough to swing an axe. He helped his pa fell trees and saw up logs to build a cabin . . . and then cut down more trees, dig out the stumps to make open fields, and grow food from the raw soil, day after day, from dawn till dusk. **If the farm failed, they would starve**.

Thomas Lincoln wanted his son to follow in his footsteps. Even aged seven, Abe wasn't so sure about that. But for now, he didn't have a choice. By law, his father **practically owned him** until he was 21: Abe had to do what he was told, hand over any money he earned, and obey his pa's orders or face a whipping.

A Shot To The Heart

The Indiana forest was a dangerous place, full of **wolves, bears and mountain lions**. Thomas Lincoln wanted his son to be able to defend himself, so when Abe was eight years old his pa taught him to shoot.

One day, when Abe was at home on his own, he saw a flock of wild turkeys in the clearing outside the cabin. Eager to impress his pa, Abe picked up his gun, aimed through a chink in the wall and shot the biggest turkey in the flock.

He ran outside to fetch his kill, heart beating with pride. But the closer he got to the turkey, the worse he began to feel. The bird looked magnificent, with its proud plumage and bright colours. **Abe was horrified** that he'd killed it. Looking down at the dead bird, he made a decision: shooting animals was definitely not for him.

Needless to say, this did not impress his pa.

That night, Abe made another decision. There was more to life than forests and farming. He'd learn everything he could about the world beyond the pinewoods . . . then when the time came to escape, he'd be ready. **No way did he want to turn out like his father**.

Life Gets Even Tougher

Abe and his family had been in Indiana for a year when his mother's foster parents, Elizabeth and Thomas Sparrow, came to live with them, along with cousin Dennis, who was now eighteen.

Dennis and Abe got along just fine now that Abe was older. Dennis helped him work around the farm and Abe kept Dennis entertained – he was a great storyteller – but just as the two boys were becoming firm friends, tragedy struck.

It was called milk sickness. No one knew where it came from, and **there was no cure**. Everyone in the little Lincoln homestead was terrified when the Sparrows caught the disease. First you got the shakes. Next came dizziness, vomiting and a racing heartbeat. Then – death.

Abe's ma was devastated at the loss of her foster parents. But just over a week later, she got the shakes herself. Knowing the end was coming, she called Abe and his sister, Sarah, to her bedside. 'I am going away from you, children,' she said, 'and I shall not return. Be good and kind to each other, and to your father, and to the world.'

Seven days later **she was dead**.

Abe, Sarah and Dennis were grief-stricken, and they only had each other for comfort. Abe's pa had no idea how to take care of a family. In the wild forest, being a mother was a highly skilled job – cooking, cleaning, making and mending clothes, curing ailments, preserving food for the winter . . . Nancy's love had held the family together. Now their lives went to ruin.

Even Abe's pa realized things couldn't go on like this, and eventually, he came up with a practical solution: he'd head back to Kentucky to **find a new wife**.

Their pa was gone for months, leaving the children to fend for themselves. Now life was absolutely desperate. Abe and Dennis did their best to farm the land and hunt for food, while Sarah tried to fill in for their ma, but she was only eleven!

Thomas Lincoln had never shown much love for his son. Sometimes, Abe wondered if he would ever return.

Sometimes, I wondered if I wanted him to!

THE DREADED STEPMOTHER

As the months rolled by, Abe wondered how life might change if his pa did come back. He and Sarah would lie awake at night, imagining what their stepmother might be like . . .

She'll be all whiskers and warts!

Then, one day, a wagon came crashing and creaking along the overgrown trail.

The first thing Abe noticed was the strong-faced lady in a tight lace cap sitting next to his pa on the driver's box. Three children's faces were poking out of the wagon behind her.

Thomas Lincoln led his new wife into his cabin to introduce her to his children. **Abe gulped**. She was coming towards him.

'Abe, isn't it?'

He nodded.

She looked down at him, eyes narrowed. 'Wait there.' She bustled out of the cabin.

Abe was imagining the worst. When she reappeared in the doorway carrying a package, he was ready to turn tail and run.

'Here,' she said. 'Open it.'

Hands trembling, Abe did as he was told.

Abe had always loved stories – they were a welcome escape from real life – but until now his book supply had been . . . limited.

Now, Abe had a way to escape his life whenever he wanted to. He devoured all the stories in the books

Sarah brought, then went on the hunt for more. It wasn't easy: there were no bookshops or libraries in the pinewoods, and Abe had to make his own lamps out of bark and grease to carry on reading after dark. To make matters worse, his pa **hated the idea** of having a bookworm for a son. Thomas Lincoln wasn't bothered that he couldn't read and write – he valued toughness above all else. At the age of six, he'd seen his own pa **murdered right in front of him**, so maybe he had good reason.

But Abe never gave up. He loved reading so much that he once walked 32 miles to borrow a book from a neighbour. When the book got soaked in the rain, the neighbour made Abe pay him back by harvesting corn for two days. Abe did the work, but then he got his revenge – by writing **rude songs** about the man's nose!

If reading had taught him one thing, it was this: words have power.

Abe's School Year

Sarah Bush Lincoln changed Abe's life for the better in lots of ways. She made new clothes for him and his sister and loved them just like her own children. She even persuaded Abe's pa to add some luxury touches to the cabin – like windows, a floor, and a proper roof!

And she saw something special in her dreamy stepson, who always had his nose in a book.

Shortly after she arrived at the Lincoln homestead, Sarah announced something that made Abe's heart leap: **she'd enrolled him at the local school**.

Abe hadn't had any schooling since leaving Kentucky. You might think that two years off learning would be every boy's dream, but Abe had spent those years slaving away on the farm. After that, lessons were a welcome break!

He built himself a cabinet for his books and wrote down his favourite bits in a homemade scrapbook, and then on the cabin walls when he ran out of pages. He memorized stories too, and told them to his schoolmates. Soon, people were coming from miles around to hear him . . .

Surprise, surprise, his pa was less impressed. The farm wasn't making enough money and the family were getting into debt. From the age of 13, Abe had to spend any spare time hiring himself out to work for the neighbours to earn some extra cash. That meant no more time for school. All in all, Abe's time in the classroom added up to **just one year**.

2   ABE'S ADVENTURES AFLOAT

Abe spent the next three years ploughing fields and splitting logs. It was hard, mindless work, but life wasn't all bad. His stepmother loved him and helped him find new books. His sister, Sarah, was clever and funny, and cousin Dennis was always good for a laugh.

When Abe was seventeen, he and Dennis hatched a plan. Fed up of chopping wood for pennies, they realized they could make much more money selling it to the riverboat captains, who needed logs to fire their engines.

Soon Abe's dream grew even bigger. With a boat of his own, he could trade along the river, see new places and make more money! He borrowed his pa's carpentry tools and built himself a neat little rowing boat. Abe was standing by the riverbank wondering how to improve his new boat, when:

Ten minutes later, Abe had the men aboard the steamer. Just as the bigger boat was about to move, Abe called up to the men: 'Hey! You forgot to pay me!'

The men reached into their pockets, and **two silver half-dollars** came spinning down, landing in the bottom of Abe's boat.

One whole dollar – that was four days' wages in under an hour! I couldn't believe it . . .

Abe's world was suddenly bursting with possibility. There were no roads and railways back then, and the Ohio River was one of America's greatest highways, forming the boundary between Indiana and Kentucky. Ferrying passengers between the steamers and the shore, Abe got to meet people from all over the country, earning big money to help his family at the same time. He had no idea **he was about to get himself into huge trouble**.

Abe was rowing along the river one day, when he heard friendly voices calling to him from the Kentucky shore. He dipped an oar and steered for the bank, where two men were waiting.

They were called the Dill brothers. They were ferrymen too, they said – but as soon as Abe stepped ashore, they suddenly seemed a lot less friendly. Grabbing him by the arms, they marched him off and had him placed under arrest! His crime? Ferrying passengers without a licence.

Abe was stunned. He'd had no idea he needed a licence, and he knew his pa couldn't afford to pay the fine. If Abe was found guilty, **he'd lose his job** and bring a whole new heap of debt on his family.

ABE'S FIRST TRIAL

On the day of his trial, Abe felt so nervous he could hardly speak. The Dill brothers were grown men, and the courthouse was packed with their friends. Abe was just a lanky 17-year-old from the wrong side of the river.

The Justice of the Peace, Samuel Pate, was nodding along as the brothers' lawyer laid out their case.

Abe couldn't afford a lawyer, of course, **so he had to speak for himself**. When his turn came at last, he took a deep breath and told the court that he'd only picked people up from his side of the river – the Indiana side. How could that be against Kentucky law?

Immediately, the Dill brothers' lawyer was on his feet. Kentucky law applied when ferrying passengers across the river from either shore, he said. To Abe's horror, Justice Pate was nodding.

Abe looked around the courtroom, desperate. There had to be a way out of this . . . *Across the river from either shore*. Could he argue the wording of the law?

Abe took a deep breath and began . . . He'd just ferried passengers to the steamers – never all the way across the river, he said. Justice Pate frowned, consulted a thick law book, and looked back at Abe with an even deeper frown.

Pate told Abe **he was right**: the law only applied if you ferried passengers all the way across the river. And with that, the case was dismissed.

Abe could hardly believe his ears. All his life, the law had been against him: it had driven his family from their home in Kentucky and it kept him bound to his pa until he was 21. Now, as he walked free from the courtroom, Abe realized that the law was just words in a book. **If you could control the words, you could control anything**.

After that, Abe had a new pastime – watching the trials in the local courthouse. It was a bit like watching an edge-of-your-seat TV series today, with heroes, villains and unexpected plot twists – except here the drama was for real. People's fates were being decided before his very eyes.

Abe had always been a joker and a storyteller, and now he became a sort of local legend – the lanky young ferryman who read Shakespeare, had won his own court case and could talk the hind leg off a donkey. After a hard day's work, people would gather at the local store to listen to his tall tales, jokes and theories about the world.

. . . farmer says, 'This is the greediest pig you'll ever see. One dollar to look at it.' So the man gives him a dollar and walks off. Farmer calls after him, 'What about the greedy pig?' And the man says, 'I saw you already.'

One of those who came to listen was James Gentry, a powerful local businessman. When Abe was 19, Gentry made him a life-changing offer.

Go South, Young Man!

Gentry was sending his son, Allen, on a trading trip to New Orleans. It was a journey of 1,300 miles downriver, so Allen was going to need some paid help. Gentry knew Abe was smart and reliable. He was offering him the job.

Abe didn't even have to think about it. Three months before, his sister had died in childbirth, aged just 20. She'd left an aching hole in his heart. Maybe this voyage would help take his mind off his grief.

The two boys set off on a misty morning in mid-April. As they poled their flatboat out onto the river and the current took hold, Abe felt a surge of excitement: at long last, **he was off to see the world**.

The current was strong, and the flatboat raced downstream. Posted at the front of the boat, Abe was constantly on the lookout for dangers ahead – sandbanks, whirlpools, sunken trees – that might appear out of nowhere.

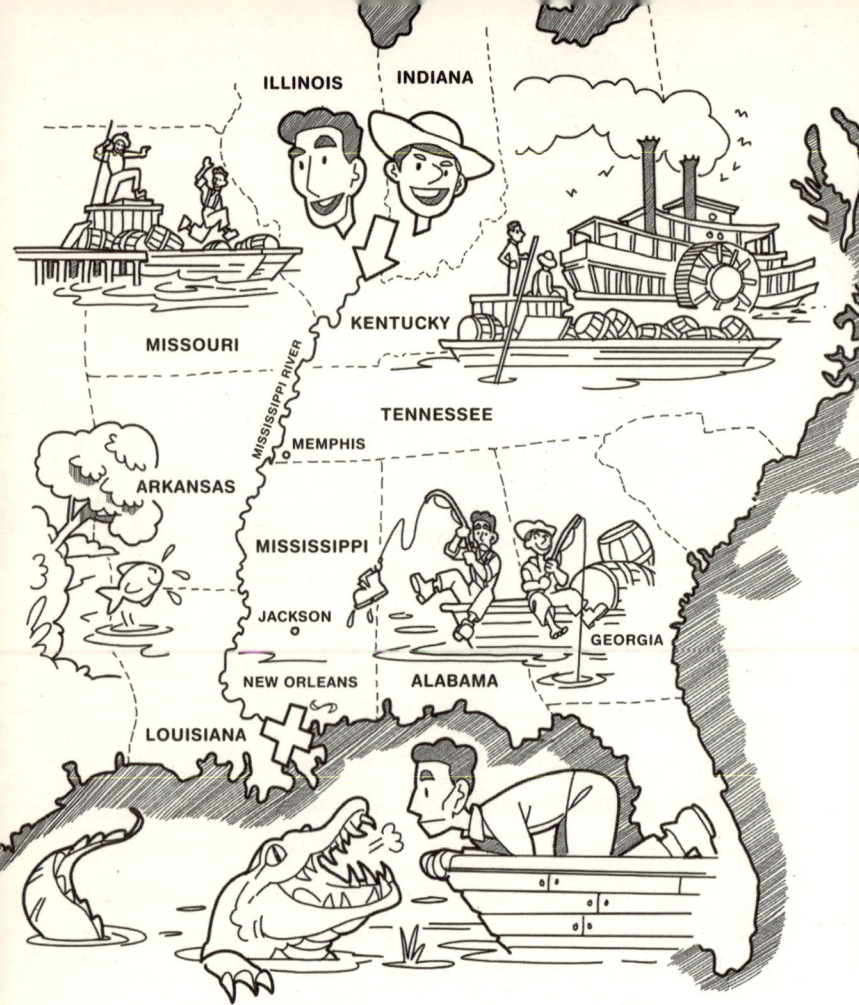

Day after day, the flatboat drifted onwards – further from home, and deeper into adventure. Abe woke up every morning feeling a little better. As they travelled south, the river got wider and busier, until one day they entered the **widest stretch of water he'd ever seen**. They were approaching the Mississippi – the greatest waterway in North America.

They moved even faster as the current picked up. Fields, houses, whole towns sped past on the distant shore. Huge steamboats passed them, churning up the water. Then, after three weeks on the river, Abe and Allen finally reached the sugar fields of Louisiana . . .

★ Sugar planters were some of the wealthiest men in America.

★ They used slave labour to harvest their sugar cane.

★ Slaves needed food to keep them going – Abe and Allen were transporting barrels of pork – vital supplies for the slaves. The planters were rich enough to pay good money for it.

Every plantation had its row of slave sheds, proudly on display. Every time Abe and Allen sold some of their cargo, slaves would come and carry it ashore. Abe had heard about slavery. Where he came from, **people called it evil**, yet here it was just a part of life. How could anyone live like that?

One evening, after a week's trading among the sugar plantations, Abe and Allen moored up on a deserted stretch of riverbank. They were just one day away from New Orleans. Everything had gone to plan, and now they could relax. Abe drifted off to sleep under the stars, looking forward to the excitement of the big city . . .

He woke with a start. Was it minutes or hours he'd been asleep? It was very dark. No sound at all from the riverbank. So why was his heart thumping so hard?

Abe lay dead still. Out on the water, a fish jumped with a plop. Then – a rustling from the shore. Something big and stealthy was moving towards the flatboat.

The rustling came again, closer this time. Slowly, not daring to breathe, Abe peered over the side of the boat – straight into the face of a black man holding a club.

The man's eyes opened wide – he shouted – then, suddenly, more men, six or seven of them, were rushing for the boat. Abe was on his feet, grappling with the leader. He'd wrestled with his friends back home more times than he could count – he was good – but this was different. **This man meant to kill him**.

Abe grabbed hold of the man's club and wrenched. The next moment it was in his hands. Whirling left and right, he drove the attackers back.

The deck was clear, but on the riverbank, they were getting ready to attack again. Spreading out, taking it slowly. Seven against two: this time, they would make no mistakes.

'Abe, get the guns!' shouted Allen.

Abe was about to reply, What guns? when he saw the men hesitate – and shouted back, 'Here, I got 'em!' instead.

Their play-acting worked. The attackers turned tail and ran.

Abe's whole body was trembling and he was bleeding. He'd never been in a fight like that. He could have killed someone or been killed himself.

'We'd better go,' said Abe. 'They might come back.'

On board the flatboat, as they paddled downstream till daylight, Abe kept seeing the face of the man he'd wrestled: the look in his eyes. It was a black face, and round here that meant one thing: **the attackers were slaves**.

Those men were on the run from a life so bad, they'd do anything to escape – even murder!

As dawn broke, Abe could see a haze of smoke on the horizon. From either bank came the sounds of steam-powered mills and factories – more and more of them, as the city drew nearer. And there was a new smell in the air – the salty, swampy tang of the Gulf Coast.

New Orleans – 'Slave City'

New Orleans was the biggest city Abe had ever seen.

It was a trading centre at the mouth of the Mississippi River that brought people together from all over the globe. Where the mighty river met the sea, different cultures mingled in a bright, swaggering carnival: French, Spanish, Mexican, Irish, Italian, American – and African. Here in the deepest South, the slave trade was alive and well, and New Orleans was its biggest market.

Abe had seen slaves by the dozen on the plantations by the river. Here, **there were thousands**. He saw them at the docks first, loading and unloading cargo. On the outskirts of town, he saw them singing and dancing to music they'd brought with them all the way from Africa.

Then, in the slave markets of the city centre, as he watched **human beings being bought and sold like animals** – stripped naked, prodded and pinched, whipped if they resisted – Abe realized that those moments of hope were like islands in a sea of misery.

Back home, when he'd had to work hard all day then hand over his earnings to his pa, Abe had often felt like a slave, but he'd always dreamed of the day he'd be free to make his own life. Now, watching children being auctioned off in the market, he realized these people would never have that chance. **They would be slaves till the day they died**.

Travelling home on a big modern steamboat, Abe had a lot on his mind. He'd seen the evil of slavery close up, and he'd never forget it.

I knew one day the time would come to put an end to it.

3   ABE STANDS AND FIGHTS

After Abe's epic journey, home seemed smaller than ever. He was still determined to escape, but just as he turned 21, his pa decided to move house again – 225 miles north-west, to Illinois.

Actually, the journey to Illinois turned out lucky for Abe when he met store-keeper Denton Offutt from the tiny village of New Salem. After Abe told Denton the story of his life so far, the store-keeper was so impressed, he **offered Abe a job on the spot**. Here, finally, was Abe's chance to leave home.

Denton's bragging brought Abe to the attention of Jack Armstrong – local wrestling champ and leader of the Clary's Grove Boys, **the toughest gang in Sangamon County**. He didn't want the new store clerk stealing his thunder, so he challenged Abe to a public wrestling contest.

Abe quickly realized he could win the fight with one well-timed throw. But humiliating the local hero in front of all his friends? Maybe not the best way to start out in New Salem . . . Mid-grapple, it's said he whispered to Jack, 'How about we call this a draw?' Armstrong knew when he was beaten and gratefully agreed.

ABE WHIGS OUT

The wrestling, storytelling grocery clerk was the new village hero – **everyone wanted to meet him**. One day, Abe looked up from his book to see a familiar figure approaching the store counter. 'The name's Green,' he told Abe, 'Bowling Green.'

Everybody in New Salem knew of Mr Bowling Green, and not just because he had a weird name. He was Justice of the Peace for the whole county, and a big cheese in local politics.

Bowling told Abe that he'd caught the eye of some important men. They'd noticed his gift for storytelling, his interest in the world and his knack for making friends with all sorts of people, and they'd decided to make him the offer of a lifetime.

READ THIS WAY
How would you like to be a Whig?
DEMOCRATS
WHIGS
ABE EXPLAINS: 'HOW TO BE A WHIG'
W
D
Not that kind of wig!
5 Each state had its own government, or General Assembly, too. They could make their own laws, raise taxes and even set up an army.
Bowling Green was offering me the chance to get elected to the General Assembly of Illinois.
VOTE WHIG
CHOOSE DEMOCRAT
6 Elections were a rowdy business. People loved them!

1 When I started out, American politics was divided into two main parties – Whigs and Democrats.
2 Whigs stood for progress – factories, schools, canals and railways – a better life for all! I liked the sound of that . . .
3 Democrats said they were for the working man . . . but they were also the party of Southern slave-owners.
4 Washington DC was where the federal government made laws for the whole of the United States.
7 Everyone had an opinion, and no one was shy about saying what they thought.
If I could just get elected to the Assembly, I could vote on new laws and raise money for those railways, schools, canals . . .

In a few months, Abe had gone from helping his family move house to running in his first election. After growing up dirt poor, stuck in the middle of nowhere, he was itching to make America a modern country where people and goods could zip from place to place using the latest transportation technology. And who knew: if all that progress spread to the South, **maybe it would even help end slavery**?

It was his chance to change the world – or the state of Illinois, at the very least.

War!

Abe was well liked around New Salem, but New Salem was just one tiny village. Abe needed votes from all over Sangamon County, where most people had never heard of him, if he was to stand a chance of winning. He had some serious travelling to do . . .

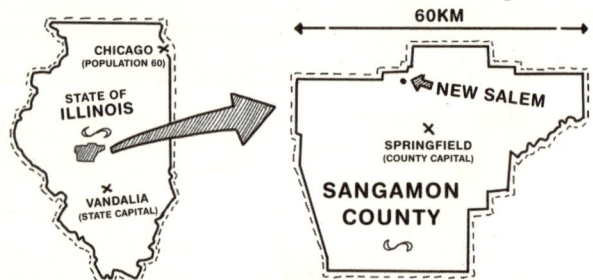

60KM

CHICAGO ✕
(POPULATION 60)

STATE OF
ILLINOIS

✕ VANDALIA
(STATE CAPITAL)

NEW SALEM

✕ SPRINGFIELD
(COUNTY CAPITAL)

SANGAMON
COUNTY

But just as Abe's campaign was getting started, a piece of news arrived that made the whole of Illinois forget all about local politics.

Black Hawk was a leader of the Native American Sauk tribe that had been driven west by white settlers years before. Now they were back to reclaim their lost lands.

As far as the state government was concerned, this was an invasion! The call went out for volunteers, and Abe jumped at the chance to defend his new home. He had no idea that most of the people in Black Hawk's 'army' were women and children. And no one seemed bothered that the tribe had been living on those lands long before the settlers had shown up.

Jack Armstrong and his Clary's Grove Boys were eager to fight too, and **they knew exactly who they wanted as their captain** . . . Abraham Lincoln.

On 29th April 1832, Abe marched out at the head of his men on a mission to hunt down Black Hawk himself. None of them had the first clue about soldiering, so it's lucky that the only Native American they met was an old Potawatomi man who was on their side anyway.

The Campaign Trail

The war was over quickly: Black Hawk's tribesmen were defeated without any help from Abe's little band of soldiers. After three months of marching to and fro in the wilderness, meeting nothing more dangerous than mosquitoes, Abe headed home with $125 (about £2,000 today) salary in his pocket – the most money he'd ever possessed.

By the time Abe got home the election was just two weeks away. When the votes were counted, it turned out **Abe had won 277 of the 300 cast** in the New Salem area, where people had heard him speak, seen him wrestle and followed him out to war. Trouble was, seeing as he'd never managed his county-wide campaign, he hardly got any votes from the rest of Sangamon County. The result? Abe came a disappointing eighth out of 13 candidates.

There were two years to wait till the next election, and meanwhile, Abe was determined to move up in the world. He spent all his new-found cash setting up a grocery store . . . which failed. With no money left, Abe had to take whatever work he could find – as a postman, farmhand, land surveyor and riverboat man. On the plus side, all these different jobs meant Abe travelled far and wide. By the time the next election came, he had friends all over Sangamon County.

Abe knew he was an odd sort of politician, with no education and no important friends or relations. But as it turned out, the voters liked a candidate who understood ordinary people and knew the meaning of hard work. They especially liked Abe's unusual campaign style.

Abe's oddball antics were such a hit, he even convinced some lifelong Democrats to vote for him. When the votes were counted on 4th August 1834, Abe had come second – but, luckily, that year Sangamon County was sending nine Whig delegates to the Assembly. **Abe's political career was about to begin.** All he needed now was some money to buy his first suit.

Hey, I charge extra for giants!

A Shaky Start

At 6 a.m. on a cold November morning in 1834, Abe boarded the stagecoach to Vandalia, the state capital, with John Stuart, a lawyer-politician who'd served alongside him in the Black Hawk War. John was an old hand at state politics, but he already respected this young man who'd come from nowhere. The two friends had plenty to talk about – which was lucky seeing as **the journey took 34 hours**!

If Abe was expecting the capital of Illinois to be a grand shining city, he was in for a big disappointment. Vandalia had only existed for 15 years. Everything in the town had been built in a hurry – including the State Capitol building.

On his first day at the General Assembly, Abe had to walk up a rickety flight of stairs to a room with bulging walls, sagging floors and a drooping ceiling. From time to time, speakers would be interrupted by chunks of plaster falling to the floor, which was already dotted with boxes for men to spit their thick, brown, smelly tobacco juice into.

Aged 25, Abe was the second youngest there and, surrounded by men who'd been in government half their lives, **he was too nervous to speak**. Thankfully, John Stuart was happy to show him the ropes. After work, Abe joined John and his lawyer friends for long evenings in the taverns, talking politics, swapping jokes and gossiping about their latest trials.

John and his friends were nothing like the people Abe had grown up with, and at first Abe felt shy around them. But that didn't last, and within a month he was speaking up in the Assembly too, putting his sense of humour to good use in solving disagreements. Abe knew **when people started laughing, they usually stopped arguing**.

The older assemblymen were so impressed by Abe that even the Democrats started asking him to speak on important matters. He campaigned for new railways and canals and spoke out against slavery. In his second term at the Assembly, he even teamed up with John Stuart and the other delegates from Sangamon to make Springfield, in their home county, the new state capital. This meant more money and power would flow into Sangamon County than ever before. Needless to say, Abe's voters were delighted!

The Assembly sat in a three-month-long session every other year. By the end of his first session, in February 1835, Abe had begun to make a name for himself.

Just my luck, though - disaster was lurking round the corner . . .

Honest Abe

Remember that grocery store that failed and swallowed up Abe's $125? Abe came home to New Salem to discover his business partner in the store had died, leaving behind debts of $1,100 (over £17,500 today). Why should that bother Abe? Well, the law said that because they'd once been partners, **Abe now had to pay back half of the debt**.

No one would have blamed Abe if he'd tried to duck out – but Abe knew and liked many of the people the money was owed to. They'd voted for him: he'd worked hard to win their trust. Even if it took him years, he decided, he'd pay back not just his half of the debt, but **the entire sum** . . . First, though, he'd have to find a very well-paid job on top of his work in the Assembly.

Ever since his ferryboat trial, Abe had been interested in the law, and now John Stuart offered him the use of his private library to help with his studies. OK, so John lived in Springfield, which was 20 miles from New Salem . . . but Abe would happily walk the distance to borrow a book or two.

It'll only take seven hours.

With no law school in the whole state of Illinois, and no actual lawyers in New Salem, **Abe had to teach himself everything**. He was a quick learner, though, and long before he'd got his official licence he was allowed to earn money arguing cases in front of the Justice of the Peace – his old friend, Bowling Green.

When people saw how hard he was working to pay off his debt, Abe won himself a nickname that would stick for the rest of his life – Honest Abe.

And it sure came in useful over the years . . .

4   Legal Eagle Abe

It was a bright afternoon in April 1837. Abe had just completed his second term at the General Assembly; he'd also got his law licence, and he even had a job lined up in John Stuart's office. But as he rode into Springfield's muddy town square on a borrowed horse, with everything he owned in the saddlebags, he knew he was taking a huge gamble. He was leaving New Salem for a new life in Springfield.

If he made it here, he could pay back his debts, boost his reputation (and his meagre income) and advance as a politician. **If he failed, he'd be penniless and disgraced**.

Right then Abe didn't even have a bed for the night – so his first stop was the general store, to buy a mattress, sheets and a pillow. When the storekeeper, Joshua F. Speed, told him the goods would cost $17 (£350 today), Abe's heart sank. He just didn't have the money.

Abe and Joshua had never met, but it just so happened that Joshua had heard Abe give a speech the year before. He'd been impressed. Seeing Abe now, down-hearted and penniless, he offered to share his own room above the shop. Abe was delighted and ran upstairs with his bags. Within minutes of arriving, he had a new home and a new friend.

Well, Speed, I am moved!

That was speedy...

Joshua Speed's store was a gathering place where friends sat around the stove talking late into the night. Abe was soon mixing with educated, well-mannered gentlemen – like the dapper Democrat politician, Stephen Douglas. Abe and Stephen already knew each other from the General Assembly, where they were both doing rather well.

Like Abe, Stephen was a risk-taker who'd struck out on his own, arriving in Springfield with five dollars in his pocket, determined to become a successful lawyer; but in other ways they couldn't be more different . . .

STEPHEN
Short, plump and always smartly dressed.

ABE
Tall, gangly and usually dressed like a scarecrow.

It had been easy enough finding friends and a place to stay, but if Abe thought he was about to earn hundreds of dollars, **he was in for a shock**. John Stuart wasn't ready to let his junior partner loose on important cases – yet.

Abe's first trials were about things like . . .

Hog debt.

You owe me $3 for that hog!

Oven damages.

You dented my stove!

Never did!

Flour power.

This here is some superfine flour!

It's ordinary.

Superfine!

Ordinary!

One year in, his debts as enormous as ever, Abe was seriously worried... Then, in March 1838, John Stuart finally decided he was ready for the big time.

Abe's First Murder

John had been hired to defend a local politician named Henry Truett, who was on trial for murder. He'd shot a man in a Springfield hotel, and **everyone knew he'd done it**. Truett's only defence was that the man had insulted him first, and then attacked him... with a chair.

It was a REALLY BIG chair, OK?

All in all, the odds were stacked against Henry – so John Stuart was taking quite a gamble letting Abe make the final speech to the jury.

Abe knew this was serious stuff. Henry had killed a man, and if the jury decided it was murder, **he would hang**. Guilty or not, Abe's job was to save this man's life. If that wasn't enough to make him sweat, he was up against his friend Stephen Douglas, one of the sharpest lawyers in town.

For weeks, Abe toiled over his speech. He could see a way he might just win. OK, so Stephen came from a better family, he'd been to better schools, spoke with a better accent . . . but did he understand Illinois people the way Abe did? Abe thought about his pa, or Jack Armstrong – any of the other hard Western men he'd known all his life – the sort of men who would make up the jury . . .

On the other hand, Stephen knew the facts were on his side, and in his speech to the jury he milked them for all they were worth. How Henry had fled the scene after the shooting – a clear sign of guilt. How the murdered man had taken days to die, his family gathered round him – he'd even accused Henry with his final breath. Up in the gallery, someone sobbed.

Now it was Abe's turn. He took a deep breath and got to his feet. **He was about to risk a man's life on a hunch**. For the hundredth time, he looked over the 12 men in the jury box – hard men, men of the West, where violence was part of everyday life.

I hope this works!

Stephen's speech had been long and flowery. Abe kept his short and simple. Henry had killed a man; there was no doubt about that. **But was it murder, or self-defence**? Abe asked the jury to put themselves in Henry's shoes – angry, insulted, and then attacked. In the heat of the moment, how would they have reacted? As Abe sat down, Henry Truett's face was ashen.

The next day, the jury returned their verdict: not guilty. Abe had earned himself $250 (over £6,000 today), impressed his boss and saved a man's life.

Frontier Kings

Now he knew he could handle them, John Stuart started sending more big-money cases Abe's way. Finally, Abe could start making a serious dent in his debts – and a serious reputation for himself.

Believe it or not, in those days, successful lawyers were superstars, known far and wide for their brilliant speeches. Imagine: you live in the middle of nowhere, with nothing to talk about but your neighbours' secrets and quarrels . . . and then one day, a bunch of fancy gentlemen ride into town to judge the whole lot of them! It was guaranteed to draw a crowd: **there was even a travelling circus** that followed Abe and his fellow lawyers around to take advantage of the ready-made audience.

A star lawyer's celebrity status could make a huge difference to how they got on in politics, and in the summer of 1838, John Stuart took a big step up when he decided to run for Congress – part of the federal government in Washington, which helped run all 26 states of America.

Now turn the book 90 degrees to your right.

55

Moving On Up!
Wondering how you run one country made up of 26 states? (I hear it's even more now!) Well . . . it's complicated.
Start reading from the bottom of the page to the top.
THE PRESIDENT
The president was top dog, but even he couldn't start a war or make a new law without agreement from Congress. Overall, the system was designed so that no one could ever get too powerful and lord it over everyone else.
SENATE
ELECTED BY ASSEMBLY FROM HOME STATE
CONGRESS

ELECTIONS

HOUSE OF REPRESENTATIVES
ELECTED BY THE VOTERS

In Washington, the two houses of Congress – the Senate and the House of Representatives – could propose new federal laws and vote on which ones to accept. Federal law applied all over the United States . . . but it wasn't supposed to affect state business. For instance, the president couldn't just order a state to abolish slavery.

STATE ASSEMBLY

State governments had power over what happened in their own state. To make a difference to the whole country, you had to head to Washington . . .

In my day, the American people elected the government . . . but not everyone got to vote: in most states women and black people were excluded.

THE PEOPLE

ELECTIONS

John Stuart was running against Abe's old friend and rival, Stephen Douglas. This election was going to be BIG, and Abe was so keen to help his boss that he wrote article after article for the local paper supporting him. People started saying Abe was the real editor of Springfield's newspaper.

When the results came in, it turned out John had won – by **just 36 votes** (out of 36,000!). Stephen was so angry he threatened to call a rematch, claiming that John and Abe had cheated. Both sides had probably bent the rules a bit, but Abe called Stephen's bluff by asking for an investigation into Stephen's campaign.

Stephen didn't like the sound of that, so he called off his challenge and John was elected. And, with John off to Washington, **Abe got a promotion**: he was now in charge of their law office.

Abe's Accidental Orchard

Being in charge meant organizing – which had never been Abe's strong point. He tried writing 'notes to self' to help him remember things. He usually kept them in his hat, along with letters, bills and other important documents. He once apologized to a client for not answering an important letter in time. His excuse . . . ? He'd recently bought a new hat.

It wasn't long before the entire office was a crazy

maze of books and papers. Abe never swept up either, and soon there was **a thick layer of dirt** in every corner. He loved to eat apples, but when he finished them he'd just toss the core over his shoulder. With the combination of dirt and apple seeds, tiny trees began to grow around him.

How's business, Abe?

Fruitful!

People could see Abe was untidy just by looking at him, but as soon as he opened his mouth, they could also tell **he had a brilliant mind**. That was what mattered most in court. And with John gone, Abe was soon taking on more cases than ever.

By 1840, Abe was known throughout Illinois as a man to have on your side, whether you were fighting an election or a murder trial. In the three years since he'd ridden into Springfield with whatever he could cram in his saddlebags, he'd built himself up into a brilliant lawyer-politician, paid off most of his debts, and was now earning a pleasing $1,500 a year (over £21,000 today).

If you think Abe was satisfied with how far he'd come, you'd be wrong. **This was just the beginning**. Meanwhile, Abe was about to fall in love . . .

Interlude - Abe And Mary

Abe was happy to sit reading by the fire in the evenings, but his good friend Joshua Speed was always dragging him along to fancy parties. Out of his depth from the start, Abe had no idea how to talk to ladies. The night he met Mary Todd, however, he knew he had to get her attention.

Mary was young, intelligent and glamorous: plenty of men were eager for her company, including Abe's rival, Stephen Douglas.

I badly want to dance with you.

Well, you're certainly dancing badly!

Him again!

Abe may have been the ugly son of a dirt-poor farmer, but he and Mary had plenty in common. They shared a love of poetry and the Whig party . . . she even liked his jokes!

But everyone else thought the pair were a terrible mismatch. Eventually, even Abe thought Mary might be better off without him, and he **stopped seeing her for a whole year**. But that year was so miserable, he decided he had to win her back . . . with a romantic gift:

Thank you . . . er, what is it?

It's the list of everyone who voted for me in the last three elections.

Oh!

The idea wasn't as daft as it sounds. Mary loved politics, but women couldn't even vote at the time, let alone govern. Mary's only hope to influence politics was to marry a man who shared her beliefs and could make it to the top – and she reckoned that might just be Abe.

On 4th November 1842, Abe and Mary announced their intention to marry. They didn't hang about: the ceremony was **that same evening**, and, nine months later, Mary gave birth to their first child, Robert.

Nine months after that, they moved into a beautiful new house, and before long, a second son, Eddie, was on the way. Remembering his own unhappy childhood, Abe was determined to be a very different kind of dad.

5   Abe Goes To Washington

By 1842, Abe had served four terms in the General Assembly and was a leading man in the Illinois Whig party. When his old boss, John Stuart, said he wouldn't be running for Congress again, Abe was eager to step into his shoes.

It took four long years, but in August 1846 Abe got a shot at the congressional election – and won with **the biggest Whig majority** the district had ever seen.

Unfinished City

Now with a wife and family in tow, the journey to Washington was a long one, and, when they finally arrived, they found that the city they'd heard so much about **wasn't quite finished**, with avenues leading nowhere and miles of roadway without houses. Everyone had cows, pigs and geese, which wandered the filthy streets during the daytime, annoying the residents.

In Springfield, 'hog menace' was one of the town's biggest problems, but other things Abe saw in Washington would take some getting used to, like the fact that **slaves were sold on the streets** here (Abe hated that).

But in contrast to the squalor, **his new workplace was magnificent**. OK, so the Capitol building was still under construction, but it contained the Library of Congress – the greatest library in the land, and Abe quickly became one of its biggest borrowers. But there wasn't much time for reading: he was here on a mission, and he was itching to get started . . .

Spotty Lincoln

The subject on everyone's lips at the time was the war between the US and Mexico, which had been raging for two long years. America was winning, and Democrat President Polk looked all set to snatch huge amounts of land from the Mexicans. Some politicians (including Abe) thought that was just plain theft.

President Polk claimed that the Mexicans had started the war, but Abe didn't believe it. Jumping in with both feet, he used his legal expertise to expose the president's lies, demanding to know the **exact spot** on American soil where the Mexicans had shed the first blood. If the president couldn't name it, how could he say the Mexicans had invaded first?

> The president is a bewildered, confounded, miserable liar . . . with blood on his hands!

> How dare he?

> Who does he think he is?

> What a hero!

Abe's attacks were shockingly bold, but they seemed to be paying off . . . at first. Then, just when it looked like the vote would go against stealing land from the Mexicans, news came that the war had been won! America had just conquered more than half of Mexico. The public went crazy with excitement, and suddenly, **opposing the war went seriously out of fashion**.

Just as he'd planned, Abe had made a name for himself with his anti-war speeches – but not in a good way. No one wanted to believe that America's great victory had been won through lies and aggression, and Abe's question about 'the exact spot' earned him a new nickname – Spotty Lincoln.

Back in Illinois, where many men had fought and

died in the war, Abe's reputation was in tatters. One newspaper claimed:

ILLINOIS STATE REGISTER

ABE LINCOLN: DIED OF SPOTTED FEVER

Of course, I was still alive, but my career in politics looked as dead as a doornail!

THE NORTH-SOUTH DIVIDE

All this new territory came with one big question: **would slavery be allowed there, or not**? Abe was horrified to think America might let it spread even further!

America had always been divided over slavery, but in 1820 the two sides drew a line on the map, and agreed slavery would only be allowed to the south of it.

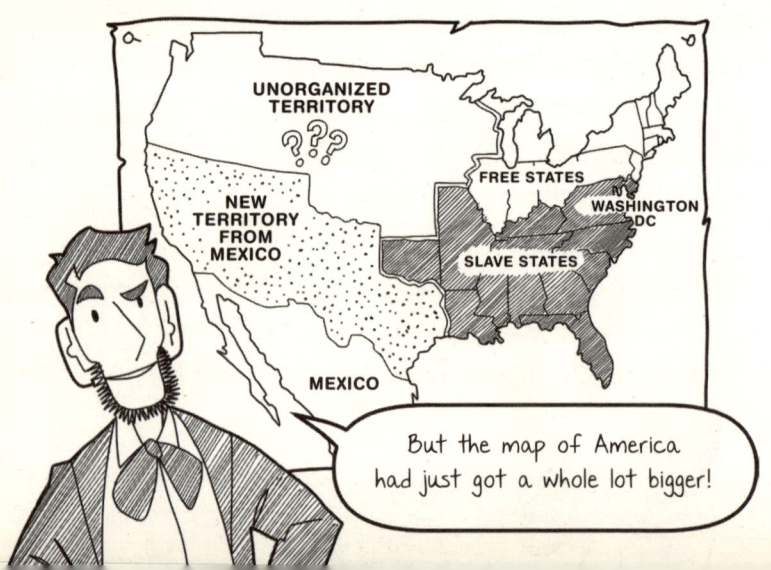

But the map of America had just got a whole lot bigger!

We banned slavery years ago.
And we don't want you Southern slave-owners gobbling up all that new Mexican land.
Northerners
Abolitionist
Southerners
In any case, slavery is plain evil and wrong. It should be banned everywhere, immediately.
What's wrong with slavery?
I agree with him.
Nobody ever asks us
We fought and died for these territories too. Why shouldn't we settle the land and take our slaves with us?

The Whigs had already tried to ban slavery from the newly conquered territories, but the Democrats had blocked the law.

Disagreements on both sides were so strong, an agreement seemed impossible.

> People started to worry that it could lead to a civil war.

WILLIAM THE WONDER-WHIG

With a presidential election coming up, Abe spent September of 1848 travelling through New England campaigning for Zachary Taylor, a hero of the Mexican war. Backing a war hero helped Abe overcome the 'Spotty Lincoln' nickname, and his speech-making did the rest: **his tour was a roaring success**, and Boston – the greatest city in New England – was going to be the high point.

Tremont Temple, Boston's biggest meeting place, wasn't just big, it was enormous. The hall of the Temple was rustling with excitement as Abe took his seat. So far he'd had audiences cheering him everywhere he went; but today, there was a much bigger name in town – the star of the Whig party and hero of the anti-slavery movement, William Seward.

WILLIAM SEWARD

William was one of those people who seemed to succeed at everything.

★ As a child, some of his friends were black `slave children`. One day, one of them ran away after a whipping and was dragged back, in chains and an iron collar, for an even worse beating. William was horrified. From that day on, he hated slavery.

★ He went on to graduate top of his class at college and was a school headmaster by the age of 17!

★ Aged 37 he ran for Governor of New York State ... and won.

★ As governor, he built schools for black children and defended the rights of slaves who'd escaped from the South.

> Why shouldn't black people have the same opportunities as everyone else?

★ He defended black people's rights, which made him plenty of enemies ...

> To me and his other supporters, he was a true American hero.

As soon as William started talking, Abe knew his speech was going to be mind-blowing. He'd listened to plenty of Whig speeches over the last few weeks, and hardly any had mentioned slavery: **it was much too dangerous**. Shockingly, William was making it the centre of his speech. He told the crowd that Zack Taylor would stop slavery spreading into the new territories. Then, as Abe listened in astonishment, William tackled the most dangerous topic imaginable. Sure, he said, Zack was a good candidate – for now – but **he was also a slave-owner**.

The time will soon come when the people want to end slavery throughout this land! Then they will demand a president who is not a slaveholder, but a freeman of the North!

I want to be like him!

That Will Seward tells it like it is!

After William had finished, it was Abe's turn to speak. He did a good job, as usual: made people laugh and scored plenty of hits against Zack Taylor's enemies. But as he spoke, Abe couldn't shake the feeling that by not mentioning slavery, he was leaving out the most important question of all.

The applause at the end was deafening, as usual. But as Abe walked off the stage, there was only one person in the room whose opinion he really cared about.

That night, the local hotels were full to bursting and, by chance, Abe ended up crammed into a small room with William! They were two very different characters. Abe was naturally shy around strangers, while **William loved a party**. He swore, drank brandy and smoked cigars all night – and he told Abe exactly what he thought about people who stayed silent on slavery.

The two of them got along like a house on fire.

Abe For Freedom...

That November, Zachary Taylor won the presidency. Abe had worked hard to make it happen, but now it didn't feel like enough. Back in Washington DC, the nation's capital, slaves were still being sold in the streets. Abe knew that even a president couldn't force the Southern states to give up slavery. But if he could start by making the change in Washington, maybe other states would follow . . .

Note to self: DO SOMETHING!!

Abe was only a junior Congressman, and he'd already got into trouble for giving President Polk a hard time. This time, he'd have to move carefully. He'd start by trying to win over the slave-owners themselves . . .

Abe put himself in their shoes. As far as they were concerned, their slaves were their property. If the government suddenly freed them all, it would be nothing short of theft! **There had to be a bit of give and take**. The mighty British Empire had freed all its slaves a few years before and the slaveholders hadn't minded too much because the government had paid them back for their lost 'property'. Maybe that could work here too.

Abe started quietly suggesting this idea to his friends in Congress. The first signs were good. Even pro-slavery Congressmen thought **the idea could work**.

Abe's term as Congressman was coming to an end, but he thought he could get his law passed in time . . . and then the anti-slavery lobby got wind of his plan.

Abolitionist

Slave-owner

Wait, you're going to pay them money to give up their slaves?

What's wrong with that?

We should be freeing *all* slaves, not just the ones in Washington!

Hey, that wasn't part of the deal!

You're on his side!

In the end, Abe got nothing but grief from both sides. After all these years, he had finally started to make his mark – then **he'd blown it**. He was forty years old and a failed politician. He'd always dreamed of changing the world: now it looked like that would never happen.

6   Abe Bounces Back

Abe pretty much gave up on politics after his failure as a Congressman. Back in Springfield, with Mary and their two sons, he settled into family life. He still had his books and plenty of good friends. Maybe he wasn't going to change the world, but at least he'd do what he could for his little corner of it.

But in February 1850, a year after he'd returned from Washington, **tragedy struck**. Abe and Mary's son Eddie died – he was only three. Abe was so bowed down by grief he sometimes felt like giving up completely – but he still had to support the rest of his family. He went back to practising law, roaming hundreds of miles to bring justice to the far-flung prairie settlements.

History of the United States, Volume Five. Hmm, it's a gripping read.

After his failed political battles, Abe now decided to become a sort of **peacemaker**, often advising his clients to 'kiss and make up'. It was a cheap solution (they didn't have to pay the cost of going to court) and it often saved friendships – even if it lost Abe money in trial fees.

THE UNSCRATCHABLE ITCH

Over the next few years, Mary gave birth to two more sons, Willie and Thomas (nicknamed 'Tad', short for Tadpole, because he never stopped wriggling). Having new babies around the house helped Abe and Mary overcome their grief. Life could have been a whole lot worse – but **there was always that little itch** at the back of Abe's mind . . .

> What if I die without changing the world even a little bit . . . ?

Abe's itch got itchier still whenever he heard how well his old rival Stephen Douglas was doing as a Democrat senator for Illinois. Each time Abe read about Stephen's success, it rubbed his own failure in a little deeper.

The question of slavery in the new territories hadn't gone away. Southern states were threatening to split off from the United States and **set up their own country** if they didn't get their way. No one wanted that, so when Stephen came up with a solution, politicians on both sides hailed it a triumph. Stephen was suggesting that the people in the new territories should vote on the matter themselves.

Abe might have been ever so slightly jealous, but he was also more than a little worried that Stephen's 'compromise' would actually encourage slavery in the new lands and make the situation even worse.

The Last Straw

Spring, 1854 – the middle of nowhere – Illinois

Abe had been riding the law circuit for weeks: it was days since he'd last seen a newspaper. So when he heard the news, it came like a thunderbolt out of a clear blue sky.

It seemed Stephen Douglas had come up with yet another 'compromise' – now the territories of Kansas and Nebraska were going to vote on whether to allow slavery. But these two states were on Northern soil – free soil. **What if they voted yes**? The North would no longer be free, and then slavery could spread anywhere.

Abe read the story in horror, then he and his fellow lawyers talked late into the night. While the rest fell asleep, Abe stayed awake, lost in thought. By the time dawn broke, he'd come to a decision.

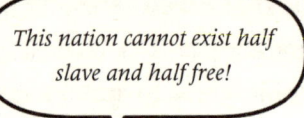

This nation cannot exist half slave and half free!

After five years away from politics, Abe felt he had to go back. He travelled all over Illinois speaking against slavery. Everywhere he went, his audiences could see just how deep his feelings were. His voice would start off quiet, then get stronger and stronger as his whole body swayed with passion. People watching couldn't help being carried along.

Abe wasn't the only one getting fired up: anti-slavery politicians all over America had set up a new party, the Republicans, to stop the spread of slavery. Abe was reluctant to abandon the Whigs, but in the end **he just had to sign up**. He even helped organize a Republican convention in Bloomington, Illinois, and gave the closing speech himself.

It was a knockout. The crowd hung on his every word. People said it was the best speech they'd ever heard. Even the reporters in the audience were spellbound. In fact, they were so amazed by it, **they completely forgot to write it down**! Even today, we have absolutely no idea what Abe said.

That was brilliant!

But what did he say?

Er . . .

Abe's speech was such a hit, he quickly became the most important Republican in Illinois, leading the fight against Stephen Douglas's pro-slavery Democrats. There was a Senate election coming up. If Abe could just defeat Stephen, it would strike a major blow in the battle against slavery.

While Stephen Douglas was well known throughout America, hardly anyone had heard of Abe outside of Illinois. Brilliantly, Abe came up with a plan to use Stephen's fame to his own advantage: he challenged Stephen to a series of seven public head-to-head debates.

ABE VS STEPHEN

While Abe travelled the hundreds of miles between debates in packed public trains, Stephen had a special train with a cannon mounted on it that **fired salutes in his honour**.

Abe turned up to debates in farmers' wagons; Stephen liked to arrive in a **fancy carriage** drawn by four white horses.

In debate number one, Stephen called Abe a failed shopkeeper, attacked his old anti-war speeches, and accused him of planning to bring thousands of black people into Illinois. That scared people – and Stephen knew it. Many of the citizens of Illinois had **never seen a black person** before.

Abe fought back with his secret weapon: his sense of humour. He made jokes at his own expense and at Stephen's, and soon he had the whole crowd in stitches.

When it came to slavery, though, Abe got deadly serious. The matter wasn't complicated, as Stephen liked to make out. Abe boiled it down to one simple question.

Is a black person a human being, or not?

Yes, of course!

Then it must be wrong to treat black people like animals.

At the end of the debate, Abe's supporters swarmed the stage, hoisted him up and passed him from hand to hand over their heads. This was Abe's first taste of **crowd surfing**, but he'd have to get used to it: his fans just couldn't help themselves . . .

They keep sweeping me off my feet!

Exactly as Abe had hoped, the debates became a national sensation. Thousands came to watch Abe and Stephen battle it out. Millions read their words in the newspapers.

By the end of the contest, Abe had travelled a whopping 4,350 miles and performed in front of tens of thousands of people. He'd loved every minute of it, and the people had loved him too. Everywhere he went, they flocked to ask questions and offer support.

When election day came on 2nd November 1858, rain was falling in Springfield. It was muddy and cold, and **voters were fighting in the streets**: the slavery issue never failed to get tempers flaring.

The result was close. Abe's Republicans had won the most votes, but Stephen's Democrats had more seats in the General Assembly. If that sounds like it doesn't add up, well, it is complicated: imagine there are ten seats in the Assembly, each with ten voters. Then suppose Abe's party wins four seats with ten out of ten votes, and loses the other six with only four votes out of ten.

Abe still ends up with only four seats, even though he's won 64 votes out of 100! That's pretty much what happened – on a much bigger scale of course – and it spelled **disaster** for Abe's Republican campaign because it was the Assembly, not the voters themselves, who got to choose the next senator.

After all the excitement, you can imagine how Abe felt. As he walked home through the rainy streets, he skidded suddenly and nearly fell face down in the mud.

Strangely, as he walked on, Abe suddenly found his mood had changed. He'd slipped – but he hadn't fallen. He'd gone up against a national celebrity, stuck up for what he believed in and so nearly beaten him. He'd made a name for himself – and now everyone in the country knew who he was, and what he stood for.

The next day, Abe opened the Illinois Gazette to read what it said about the result – and couldn't believe his eyes.

The paper's editor wasn't talking about the Senate race any more. He was talking about who should stand for the next election – **the presidential election** – and he had the ideal candidate in mind . . .

Who me?

ILLINOIS GAZETTE

. . . THE STATESMAN OF TODAY AND OF THE NEAR FUTURE – ABRAHAM LINCOLN

ABE FOR PRESIDENT!

It seemed incredible: Senate loser one day, possible candidate for the presidency the next . . . but then, these were incredible times. America was facing the biggest decision in its history: be a slave empire, or a free nation of equals. Finally, Abe had his chance to change the world – and Mary was with him all the way – but there were still a load of hurdles to jump. Abe had to persuade the national Republican party to nominate him as their candidate – and that raised a problem:

NEW YORK TIMES
WILLIAM SEWARD – THE ONLY CHOICE FOR A REPUBLICAN PRESIDENT

I was up against my hero!

Everyone expected the man who had inspired Abe all those years ago to win – even William Seward himself (things usually did go his way, after all). But while William's bold speeches had won him loads of fans, he'd made plenty of enemies too. Some Republicans worried that he would divide the country even more than it already was – and by 1859, **America was divided like never before**. Northerners hated the South for wanting to spread slavery. Southerners hated the North for wanting to get rid of it. In October 1859, a man named John Brown raided the government weapon store in the Southern town of Harper's Ferry. He planned to arm slaves with the stolen guns and start a mass rebellion. The raid was a failure, and John Brown was hanged for treason – but he faced death so bravely he became a hero in the North.

*John Brown's body lies a-mouldering in the grave
But his soul goes marching on!*

ABOLISH SLAVERY

Southerners were terrified of armed slaves coming to kill them – and they blamed Republicans like William Seward for encouraging John Brown, offering a **$50,000 reward for William Seward's head**.

What with all the tension and drama around William, Abe could see an advantage in being the 'quiet one'. He wasn't even officially in the race yet. Even if he was nominated, no one outside Illinois seriously expected him to win . . .

> . . . and the longer they kept thinking that, the better.

Abe didn't reveal his interest in running for president until 1860. After playing things cool at first, now he went on a whirlwind tour of the Eastern states, making speeches to packed audiences that would be printed up and read by thousands more people. Abe was a big name now, and when he visited his eldest son (now 17 and studying in New Hampshire, aiming to get into Harvard College), Robert's fellow students were completely in awe of his famous dad:

> Hi, Dad!
>
> You're *the* Abe Lincoln?
>
> Can I have your autograph?
>
> I've read all your speeches!

In March, with two months to go till the nomination, Abe returned to Illinois. William was still firm favourite to win, so Abe sent his supporters off on a simple quest: to speak to the other candidates' supporters and ask them to **make Abe their second choice**. That was all . . .

ABE Explains: The Republican National Convention

466 Republican delegates came from all over the country to choose their presidential candidate in front of an audience of ten thousand people. There were 13 candidates in all, and to win, one of them needed more than 50 per cent of the votes.

It took several rounds of voting!

- William Seward
  173.5
- Abraham Lincoln
  102
- Simon Cameron
- Salmon P. Chase
-
-

At the end of round one, William was in the lead by a mile.

It's too soon to celebrate, boys...

William was still 59 votes short of a majority.

Our man's third, he can't win now...

*...but they **can** switch to their second choice!*

William kept his lead in round two – just – but now it was a straight race between me and William. As candidates dropped out of the running, one by one, all those who'd promised to make me their second choice now swung my way.

Finally, in round three, I won 349 votes – a landslide victory!

When the final vote was announced, there was stunned silence for a moment. Then, with a stamping and roaring that was heard for miles around, the crowd went wild.

THE ONLY WAY IS UP

It was a fantastic moment for Abe: he was now the official Republican candidate. But the battle was only just beginning – guess who else fancied himself as president?

Just like everyone else, the Democrats had expected superstar William Seward to become the Republican candidate. When it turned out to be Abe – a weird-looking farmer's son with no experience in government – they were confident the presidency would be theirs. Democrat newspapers had a field day making fun of Abe. They called his speeches 'illiterate', his jokes 'clumsy', his brains 'fourth-rate', and his looks 'unwarrantably ugly'. Meanwhile, Abe's own party wasn't sure what to make of him. Some Republican newspapers even **had difficulty spelling his name**. There was work to be done.

ABE EXPLAINS: HIS TIPS FOR THE TOP

Presidential elections were a HUGE deal with enormous crowds, passionate speeches and nationwide campaigning. I never really expected to become the Republican candidate ... Suddenly I found myself in charge of the biggest campaign of my life! I learned a few lessons along the way:

Don't go off travelling the country to campaign; have the people come to you!

ILLINOIS GAZETTE — ABRAHAM LINCOLN FOR PRESIDENT!

Would you stop slavery in Kansas?

What was your father *really* like?

How delightful to meet you, Senator!

What about the African slave trade?

Make sure you have a great partner. The people who said I was too rough to be president soon changed their tune after they met Mary.

Keep your friendships strong: it took three months, but William got over losing to me in the end. In August 1860 he set off round the country telling everyone to vote for me!
We're both Republicans and we're in this fight to win it!
I wouldn't even be in it if it wasn't for you!
Listen to your public . . .
Dear Mr Lincoln, I'm only 11, but I think you'd look much better with a beard . . . If I was a man, I'd vote for you . . . Goodbye, Grace Bedell
Hmm.

Thousands of visitors came to see Abe, and he even wrote a short story of his life – which **sold over a million copies**! Voters loved the idea of a man born in a log cabin moving into the White House as president, and the more people got to know 'Honest Abe', the more they liked him ... though the Southern slave-owners still hated him, of course. Abe knew he would lose in the South: so he'd just have to make sure he won everywhere else ... That meant getting more brilliant speakers like William Seward on side, and making sure they said the right thing wherever they campaigned.

> New Jersey?
>
> All they care about is the steel industry.
>
> I'll rustle up the perfect speech for them!

Luckily, while Abe had been building alliances in the Republican party, Stephen's Democratic party had started falling apart and the Whigs were completely out of the picture. Stephen kept suggesting compromises, but Southern Democrats wanted someone who would fight tooth and nail to protect slavery. They refused to nominate Stephen as their candidate, and split off to fight their own campaign against both him and Abe. With his enemies divided, Abe had every reason to be optimistic – but that didn't stop him working flat out till the very last minute.

Election day finally came on 6th November 1860, and for Abe, in Springfield, it seemed to go on for ever. He sat down to a 'victory dinner' even though the results hadn't even come in yet. Everyone else was convinced Abe had won and they were keen to celebrate, but Abe was biting his nails with worry.

By midnight, the results still hadn't arrived. It was in the early hours of 7th November that the news was finally telegraphed through. The citizens of Springfield had been right to celebrate: **Abe had won**.

The parties went on till dawn.

> Even in my darkest moments, I'd always had my dreams . . . but this was way beyond the wildest of them!

Abe knew he couldn't have won without the support of his

friends and family. After he got the news, he shook free of all the crowds who'd come to congratulate him and ran through the streets of Springfield to his home.

Mary! Mary! WE are elected!!

Well, hot diggity-dee!

It was his greatest moment of triumph, but it wasn't going to last for long. The Southern states had all voted for the pro-slavery Democrats – they were horrified by Abe's win. Never mind that Abe had promised not to meddle in their business – and he'd only ever campaigned against *extending* slavery – they believed he was out to abolish slavery and destroy their way of life. They had already **vowed never to accept him as president**, and on 20th December, the state of South Carolina declared itself independent of the United States. Within two months, six more Southern states had done the same.

Abe was president – but the United States were no longer united. It was the worst crisis the country had ever faced. And it was up to Abe to sort it out.

7 Abe's Darkest Hour

Washington Railway Station, 23rd February 1861 – 6.00 a.m.

Abe arrived in Washington to begin his presidency without pomp or ceremony. No crowd had gathered to meet him, no one was there to cheer him on – and that was exactly how he wanted it! He was even wearing a disguise . . .

He hurried through the deserted station, muffled in the scarf that partly covered his face. Things had been bad for months: it was hard to ignore the country splitting in two, and now it seemed the government was riddled with Southern traitors, who'd hatched a **plot to assassinate Abe** before he'd even started his presidency. That's why he was coming to take up office secretly, like a thief in the night.

When news of Abe's secret train ride got out, he became a laughing stock. Some said he'd dressed as a woman to sneak onto the train. Others claimed he'd hidden in the cattle car dressed in his nightshirt. Abe was embarrassed – but looking ridiculous was the least of his worries. He might be

That's our president?

president in name, but he had **no experience**, there were enemies all around him, and the country was very nearly at war. Even his supporters were asking themselves whether he was really up to the job.

In At The Deep End

Desperate to avoid civil war, Abe used his first speech as president to make a moving appeal for peace. But the rebel Southern states weren't listening: they were determined to fight, and had already started preparing.

On 13th April, the rebels captured Fort Sumter in Charleston Harbour, South Carolina, where there was a garrison of loyal government soldiers. There was no turning back now: they'd fired their cannons on US troops and forced them to surrender. The American Civil War had begun. Abe had tried to prevent it – and now he was being blamed for not striking first.

Abe had always been bad at organizing things, he knew nothing about military strategy – yet here he was, in charge of what was to be **the bloodiest war ever fought on American soil** . . .

ABE Explains: The American Civil War - 1861-1865

So who was fighting who ... and why?

UNCLAIMED TERRITORIES

THE BORDER STATES.

★ These were slave states that hadn't rebelled – yet. They were still making their minds up – I'd have to work hard to keep them from joining the rebels.

THE SOUTH (aka – 'Confederates', 'rebels'.)

★ The slave states of the South had given themselves a new name: the Confederate States of America. They claimed they'd started a new country, and only wanted to be left alone ...

★ I always said they were nothing but a bunch of rebels ... but they sure knew how to fight!

THE NORTH (aka 'Yankees', 'The Union').

★ The free states of the North were loyal to me: in fact, they were all that was left of the 'United States'.

★ We had more people, factories and weapons than the rebels.

★ Everyone said we'd win easily. Well, they were wrong . . .

CIVIL WAR STATS

Developments in technology meant this war was different from any that had gone before:

★ New railways could transport armies hundreds of miles in a single day.

★ Telegraph wires could carry electrical signals 50,000 miles, so messages flew across the states at lightning speed. Abe could take charge of the war like no other leader before him.

> And when things went wrong, it was my responsibility . . .

★ Thanks to better rifles, modern artillery and the world's first machine guns, the American Civil War was deadlier than any war that had ever been fought before. In total, over 600,000 soldiers were killed.

> Progress isn't always a good thing . . .

It wasn't just Abe who was **completely unprepared** for the war. The Union army was tiny and spread out across half the continent. Washington might be the capital city, but its defences were pathetic. When the country's greatest soldier, Robert E. Lee, went off to lead the rebel army in Virginia, Abe must have been in despair.

Abe was **out of his depth** in a war he'd never wanted to fight, but he still believed it was up to him to win it; he was president and commander-in-chief, after all.

> Uh-oh!

> Mr President, the troops are held up!

> Mr President, the city is surrounded!

> Mr President, the railway's down!

He worked day and night for weeks, raising taxes to pay for a huge new army, teaching himself military strategy and trying to stop the border states from joining the rebellion. Gradually, the hard work began to pay off: thousands of fresh recruits marched down to protect the capital, and by the time the hot, humid Washington summer rolled in, the army had grown big enough to go on the attack.

Abe had read all he could on military theory, but he reckoned the actual plan of campaign should be left to the professionals – college-educated generals who knew the history of warfare back to front. None of them realized this war was going to be *totally unlike* any other ... and that the methods they'd been taught would be **worse than useless**.

Abe listened to his generals – and agreed to a bold plan of attack. The army marched south towards the railway depot at Manassas Junction, Virginia, where Southern forces were gathering. There were far more Union soldiers than rebels, and the people of Washington were so sure of victory that some of them **rode out in carriages with picnics to watch the battle**. Once the rebel army was brushed aside, the road to Richmond, their capital, would be open. The war would be over in weeks!

Abe wasn't so confident as he waited nervously at the telegraph office for news from the battlefield – thousands of men were about to risk their lives on his orders. At 4.30 in the afternoon on 21st July 1861, the result finally came through: the Union army had won a glorious victory!

As the streets thronged with cheering crowds, Abe went for a celebratory carriage ride into the countryside with his youngest son, Tad. He returned feeling better than he had in weeks. But back at the White House there was grim news waiting.

The Union hadn't won the battle after all. Just when victory looked certain, the rebels had counterattacked. **Nine thousand fresh troops** had poured out of the woods, taking the Union soldiers completely by surprise. The Union soldiers had run for it, and now a flood of soldiers, wagons, horses and terrified battle tourists were pouring back towards Washington.

> What a dreadful sight! It's put me right off my éclair.

Abe watched from the White House windows as the broken army straggled in through the night. The groans and screams of the injured broke his heart.

He'd ordered these men into battle. They'd trusted him. **He'd failed them all.**

Abe couldn't bear to stand and watch; he had to do something. He went to his desk and started scribbling. By the end of that terrible night, he had sketched out a new strategy for the entire war. And this was it:

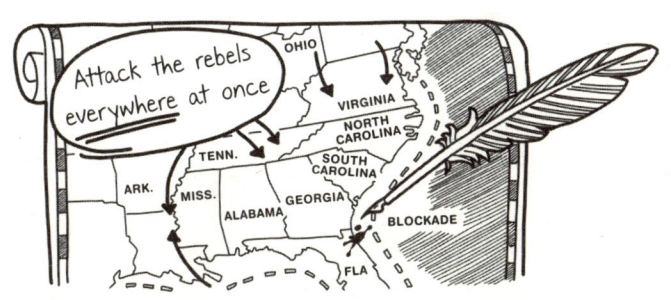

> Attack the rebels everywhere at once

Abe's plan was utterly brilliant . . . but it was up to his generals to make it happen.

The next morning, Mary was advised to leave with the children – their safety couldn't be guaranteed. She turned to Abe and asked if he was leaving. Of course, he had to stay put. In that case, Mary said:

> I'm staying too!

THINGS CAN ONLY GET BETTER . . . ?

The Lincoln children, Willie, now ten, and Tad, aged eight, were too young to feel afraid. Their older brother Robert was safe, hundreds of miles away, studying at Harvard now . . . but the younger boys didn't envy him for a moment. For them, **the war was one big adventure**. They built a fort on the roof of the White House, and sometimes interrupted Abe's meetings to invite everyone to watch a play in the attic.

In the evenings, after work, Abe let his sons run riot with their friends: visitors to the White House might find the president of the United States pinned to the floor by a pack of wild children.

> Hello there! How can I help?

As the war raged on, Mary decided to throw a lavish party to lift everyone's spirits. Then, a few days beforehand, Willie came down with a fever. Mary wanted to call off the party, but Abe knew how much it meant to her, so he summoned the best doctor in Washington to examine Willie.

The doctor was reassuring: Willie was in no immediate danger. Abe and Mary breathed a sigh of relief and went ahead with the party. But just as the guests began pouring in, news came from upstairs that **Willie had taken a turn for the worse**. Abe hoped it was a false alarm – it was too late to cancel the party.

Abe did his best to keep smiling, amid the glittering gowns and uniforms, but he couldn't wait for everyone to go home. Finally, the last of the guests left, and Abe and Mary hurried to their son's bedside.

Our poor little boy.

He's burning up with fever.

The days that followed were a living hell. Willie was getting worse. Then Tad caught the infection too. Abe and Mary watched in agony as **their sons fought for their lives**. In the end Tad recovered, but his big brother – who loved poetry and reading and was his father's favourite – was not so lucky.

Mary was inconsolable. She could hardly bear to be around Tad. Abe was bowed down by grief too, but no way could he take a break. So, everywhere he went, Tad went too – riding on his dad's shoulders as he walked between meetings, snuggling in his lap as they listened to long speeches, and following on a pony when Abe rode out to visit the troops.

The Show Must Go On

Meanwhile the war was going from bad to worse. The Union armies managed to regroup after their first shock defeat, but they just couldn't seem to win any of the battles that mattered.

In charge of the rebel army of Virginia was the brilliant Robert E. Lee, one of the best generals of all time. Union troops far outnumbered the rebels but Lee was brilliant at trickery, swift movement and unexpected attacks.

If only I could have persuaded him to fight for us!

Robert E. Lee

The Union army was led by George B. McClellan. He believed he was God's gift to soldiering and that it was his misfortune to be surrounded by idiots. Whenever there was a chance for a decisive battle, though, **George found excuse after excuse not to attack**.

George B. McClellan

By the summer of 1862, the **death toll** on both sides was in the **hundreds of thousands** and victory seemed further away than ever. The responsibility for those deaths was weighing Abe down, though, true to form, he never tried to duck it. He wrote letters to the families of the dead, finding just the right words to help them in their grief. For Abe the task was all too personal: he knew what it was like to lose those closest to him.

As the pain and the deaths mounted, Abe's resolve was flagging. He'd tried to avoid war altogether and failed. He'd lost his son. Every decision he made seemed to be the wrong one. His new military strategy might turn out to be brilliant in the end, but right now **all Abe could see was failure**. He was tired of it all – and afraid the people would give up on him. Without the people on his side, the war would be lost. All the pain would have been for nothing.

I knew something had to change – and, finally, I had an idea . . .

8   ABE'S BIG SECRET

September 1862 – the White House

At the end of another long day, Abe was leafing through the newspaper on his desk. The editor of the paper, Frederick Douglass, was angry . . . and he was specifically angry with Abe. He called the president a hypocrite and an arrogant racist who had nothing but contempt for black people.

Frederick had every right to be angry. The tale of his life made Abe's look like one long summer holiday, because Frederick was black. **He'd been born a slave**. Everyone knew his story, because after escaping to the North he had written a book describing his life as a slave. It was an incredible tale and it soon became a bestseller . . . .

> Now, finally, you might understand how we black people have suffered.

FREDERICK DOUGLASS – THE ONE THAT GOT AWAY

★ Born a slave, in around 1818, Frederick was torn from his mother's arms as a toddler, then taken from his grandmother a few years later. (A slave had to go wherever he was sent.)

★ He was taught to read by his master's wife, even though it was illegal.

★ Dreaming of escape helped him survive slavery.

★ He finally did escape in 1838. While working in a shipyard, he hopped on a train heading north and made it to New York in disguise.

★ Life in the North was better for black people, but still no bed of roses, with racist laws and slave-hunters chasing him. Frederick never forgot the millions of slaves he left behind.

★ He worked as a labourer, but began writing and travelling the country making speeches against racism and slavery.

★ After touring Great Britain and Ireland he raised so much money, he bought a printing press and set up his own newspaper.

Up until now, Frederick and his newspaper had supported Abe in the hope that, one day, Abe would help free Frederick's people. Lately, though, Abe couldn't seem to open his mouth without saying something . . . disappointing.

If I could preserve the Union without freeing a single slave, I would do it.

There was a reason for this, but Frederick didn't know it yet. For months now, Abe had been biding his time – and **nursing a very big secret** . . .

THE PROCLAMATION

Ever since the war began, people had been telling Abe what he should do about slavery. Millions in the North wanted to abolish it – but even as president, Abe could only do that if the governments of the slave-owning states agreed. What's more, plenty of Northern soldiers thought slavery was just fine. Abe had no idea how they'd react if he suddenly told them they were fighting to end it. Worst of all, the border states still had slaves, and didn't want to give them up. If Abe looked like he was going to force them to, they might join the rebels and tip the balance of the whole war.

Freeing the slaves wasn't simple, it wasn't easy, it wasn't even legal. But Abe was starting to believe it might be the only way to win.

Earlier in the summer of 1862, Abe had used all his legal cunning to write up a secret Proclamation. In July, he'd read it out to his ministers.

> On January 1st, 1863, as a necessary military measure, all persons held as slaves within any rebel state, shall then, thenceforward, and for ever, be free.

Abe had found a loophole in the law that said, during wartime, a president could do things that wouldn't be allowed in peacetime – as long as those things were necessary for victory. If the South lost its slaves, Abe thought, **who would tend the fields and work the factories**? How would it make new weapons?

How would it feed its armies? Freeing the slaves in the South would most **definitely help win the war**, Abe realized – and that made it most definitely legal!

His ministers were all flabbergasted. Only William Seward spoke up: the Proclamation could be a triumphant success, he said . . . or a terrible disaster, depending how people reacted. At that point, with the North losing battle after battle, the people's mood was looking ugly. So William gave Abe some advice:

> Whatever you do, don't tell anyone about it – yet!

One way to cheer people up was to win a big battle, William explained: so why not wait for a victory, then announce the Proclamation while everyone was celebrating? People had gone so crazy when they'd won the Mexican war, it had nearly ended Abe's career! He decided William was right. The Proclamation had to stay secret – and that was why he'd been doing his best to sound like he wasn't really interested in freeing any slaves at all.

Meanwhile, the Union armies were in trouble. As summer turned to autumn, they couldn't even turn up a little victory, let alone one Abe could call 'a triumphant success'. Now, with Frederick Douglass turning against him, Abe was beginning to wonder whether he could hang on much longer.

THE CIGARS THAT MADE HISTORY

On the rebel side, Robert E. Lee was having a whale of a time. He'd forced George McClellan's huge Union army to retreat in shame outside the rebel capital, Richmond, and he'd won another great victory at the Second Battle of Manassas. Now, he decided the time had come to capture Washington and break the North once and for all.

It was his boldest move yet, and **Abe was hoping it would also be his first big mistake**. As Lee began his invasion, Abe promised himself . . .

Note to self: if Lee is beaten, announce the Proclamation!

A few days after reading Frederick's article, Abe got news from General McClellan. One of his soldiers had found a bundle of cigars that a rebel officer had dropped. The cigars were wrapped in a grimy sheet of paper with writing scribbled all over it – this 'wrapping paper' was a copy of Robert E. Lee's order for his entire army!

Now **McClellan had his hands on the enemy's plans**, Abe wanted him to seize the chance to attack: he could wipe out Lee's army and end the war there and then! This time, even George couldn't find an excuse not to fight. As usual, though, he dithered – and by the time he finally marched his men to battle, Lee had realized his plans were missing and changed his army's position.

The result was the Battle of Antietam – the most horrifying single day in American military history, with **23,000 men killed**. The dead covered the battlefield like a carpet. In the end, the Union army claimed it as a victory, but only because they outnumbered the rebels two soldiers to one.

The rebels retreated, exhausted. Abe was furious with George for wasting the information in the cigar wrapper, and finally fired him as commander-in-chief soon afterwards. But for now, **Lee had been beaten at long last**: it was time for Abe to keep his promise to himself.

A week after the battle, Abe made his secret Proclamation public. He gave the rebels three months to stop fighting. If they didn't, on 1st January 1863 the Proclamation would become law.

The crowd outside the White House sang and cheered. The South spat with rage. But Abe was waiting for one reaction in particular. As soon as the next edition of *Douglass Monthly* was printed, he grabbed a copy, hot off the press.

'[Abraham Lincoln's] *word has gone out . . . giving joy and gladness to the friends of freedom and progress,*' Frederick wrote. *'We should shout for joy!'* Well – that was a good start.

A New Beginning?

Now he'd announced the Proclamation, Abe made one important change to it: free black men could now fight in the Union army (racist politicians had banned them from joining up back in 1792). Giving black soldiers the right to serve their country was a much-needed sign of respect. Abe was also hoping it would scare the rebels, bring the Union together and help end the war.

There was just one problem. As the weeks passed, it looked like Abe's Proclamation was doing the exact opposite.

Abe had always known the Proclamation was a gamble, and now it looked like it might end up losing him the war. If that happened, the rebel states would get to keep their slaves anyway, America would be broken in two for ever, and hundreds of thousands of men would have died for nothing. But the Proclamation wasn't legal yet. It would only become law when Abe signed it on 1st January. **There was still time to back down** . . .

When New Year's Eve came, Abe knew he wouldn't be getting any sleep. Before she went to bed, Mary gave him her view on the matter. She told him not to sign.

All night, he paced his study, thinking. He felt like a tiny cog in a huge machine. This decision was so much bigger than him. How could he possibly think it through?

As the hours passed, Abe realized that maybe he couldn't. Maybe all he could do was follow his conscience. He'd made his promise back in September, and God, or Fate, had kept their side of the pact with the Union's victory at Antietam. Maybe this decision was already out of his hands.

On the afternoon of 1st January 1863, Abe sat down with William Seward and the final copy of the Proclamation. As he lifted the pen, he realized his hand was trembling.

Abe laughed nervously. 'I've been shaking hands all morning till my arm's half numb,' he said to William. 'If the signature's unsteady, people will say I wasn't sure about this.'

William knew as well as he did just how uncertain Abe had been. Even now, it felt like a leap in the dark – but as Abe began to sign his name, **his hand stopped trembling**.

This feels right!

It was done. Abe felt a great weight lifting. He still didn't know whether the Proclamation would bring victory or defeat. But now he'd signed his name to set three million people free, he finally felt absolutely sure it was the right thing to do.

9   ABE KEEPS HIS PROMISE

News flashed along the telegraph wires, quick as lightning: Honest Abe had stuck to his word. Across the North, crowds of his supporters cheered and wept for joy as they heard the news. In the South, the slaves had no telegraph wires. They had something else: they called it the grapevine.

A slave sent on an errand to the next plantation would tell the first fellow slave he met – who passed it on, again and again, until the news had spread all across the South. The grapevine was so quick, many **slaves knew they were legally free before their masters** read it in the newspapers.

From now on, wherever the Union armies went, they were met by black men eager to fight for the freedom of all their people.

Frederick Douglass took the lead in recruiting them – and made Abe promise him that black soldiers would get the same pay as any others. Frederick, along with the 173,000 black soldiers who signed up to fight, knew exactly what this meant: if a black man could fight for his country, that made the country his. After that, America would belong to black people as much as it belonged to anyone else.

From now on, Abe and Frederick were firm friends for life.

Seeing It Through

The rebels were more outnumbered than ever. The new black soldiers swelled the Union ranks, and fought like tigers. **The tide was finally starting to turn**.

Over in the West, a general named Ulysses S. Grant captured the town of Vicksburg on the Mississippi

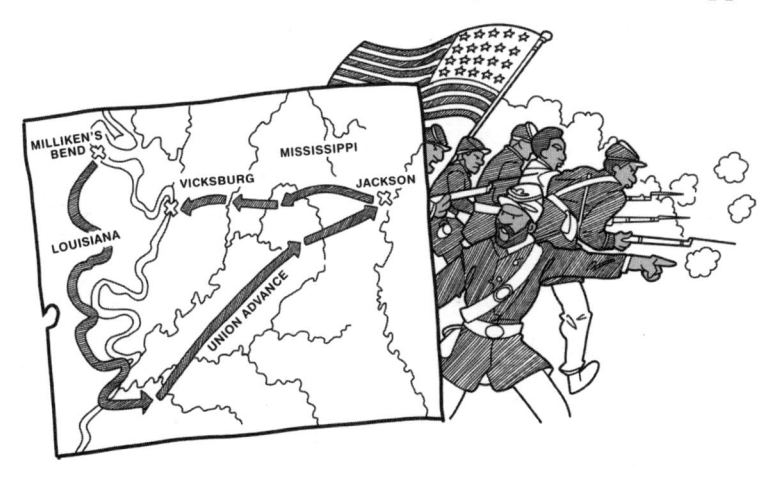

River, with the help of escaped slaves. Vicksburg opened up the Mississippi to Union forces and, suddenly, **the back door to the South was wide open**.

Gung-ho Generals

Making the civil war into a war against slavery changed everything. Now they really were fighting against the Southern way of life, and with McClellan gone, Abe had searched for a new kind of general – one who'd do whatever it took to win. Luckily, he'd found two!

Ulysses S. Grant

William Sherman

Finally! Commanders who were willing to hurt the enemy!

One-time wagon driver and stubborn as a mule. After winning in the West, Abe made him commander of all the Union armies. In spring 1864, Ulysses promised Abe he'd grind Robert E. Lee down in the East.

William wanted to get the war over with, and didn't mind fighting dirty. He ordered his soldiers to steal everything they could carry and burn anything they couldn't. He's still remembered as a villain in parts of the South today.

Grant and Sherman were two of the toughest generals America ever had. A century later, when the US army was battling the Nazis in Europe, the Allies knew exactly what to call their armoured tanks:

M3 GRANT   **M4 SHERMAN**

Since the beginning of the war, Abe's great strategy had been to attack the rebels everywhere at once, and now, at last, **that strategy was paying off**. Robert E. Lee didn't have enough men to win in the East and the West at the same time. In the end, he tried launching an invasion of the North, using his full army, instead. They got as far as Pennsylvania before the Union army caught up with them at the town of Gettysburg on 1st July 1863 . . .

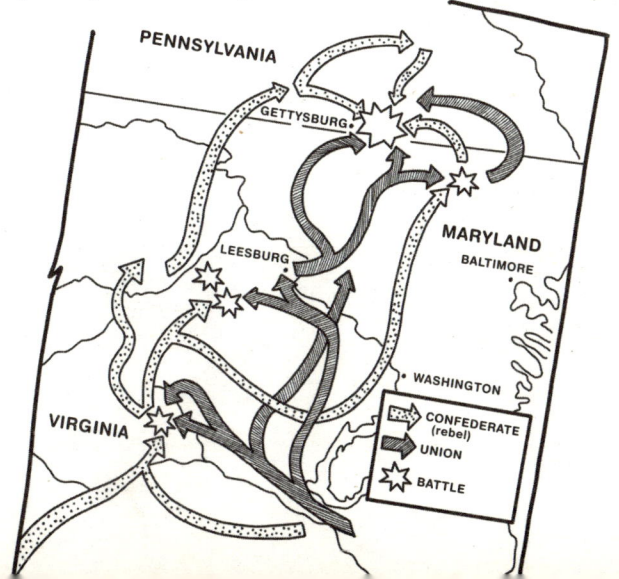

The fighting lasted three days, raging back and forth through the town, with terrible casualties on both sides. Finally, Robert E. Lee ordered over 13,000 men to mount one great assault. They were driven back by a storm of rifle and cannon fire, leaving **over 4,000 bodies** behind on the field.

After the Battle of Gettysburg, it looked like the Union was sure to win. In fact, some people were saying this was the perfect time to make the rebels an offer. Something like: 'Stop fighting, come back into the Union, and we'll let you keep your slaves.'

This was exactly what Abe didn't want. He'd promised freedom to millions of people. Black men were fighting and dying because of that promise. If he betrayed them now, they'd think he'd played a dirty and devious trick on them.

You ask why you should fight for black people? Strange — they seem willing to fight for you!

Can't argue with that.

He's got a point.

Every time he visited the frontline, Abe was amazed by the courage and spirit of the soldiers – even after the most terrible battles. He knew they would see the war through. Now he just had to convince the people to do the same.

Abe's Shortest Speech

18th November 1863 – Gettysburg

Abe was finding it very hard to concentrate. Back home, Tad was ill, and Mary was terrified of losing yet another son. So was Abe – but the speech he had to give tomorrow was seriously important; there was no way he could cancel it.

This wasn't any old visit. Abe had been invited to dedicate the Gettysburg battlefield as a graveyard for the fallen soldiers. These were men who had laid down their lives to fight for what they believed in, and they deserved the highest honour he could give them . . . he'd just **run out of time** to finish his speech.

A crowd had gathered outside the house where William Seward was staying. Abe could hear them. They wanted a speech, so William was giving them one. He was making it up as he went along, and it was brilliant! William had a way of making everything look easy.

The crowd hung around for hours, cheering and singing songs, as Abe went on writing.

The next day, **thousands of people gathered** on the battlefield to hear the dedication. Abe was on second, after Edward Everett, a famous historian.

Now if you ever want a short speech about a famous battle, here's a tip: don't ask a historian. Edward knew everything there was to know about the Battle of Gettysburg, and he seemed to include it all in his speech – which went on for two whole hours! By the end, half the audience was asleep.

When Edward finally finished, Abe stood up. It was so quiet, he could hear the boards creaking beneath his feet as he walked across the platform. Hoping the audience weren't all asleep, he put on his glasses, looked down at his notes, and cleared his throat . . .

Four score and seven years ago our fathers brought forth on this continent, a new nation, conceived in liberty, and dedicated to the proposition that all men are created equal.

Now we are engaged in a great civil war, testing whether that nation, or any nation so conceived and so dedicated, can long endure. We are met on a great battle-field of that war. We have come to dedicate a portion of that field, as a final resting place for those who here gave their lives that that nation might live. It is altogether fitting and proper that we should do this.

But, in a larger sense, we cannot dedicate – we cannot consecrate – we cannot hallow – this ground. The brave men, living and dead, who struggled here, have consecrated it, far above our poor power to add or detract.

The world will little note, nor long remember what we say here, but it can never forget what they did here. It is for us the living, rather, to be dedicated here to the unfinished work which they who fought here have thus far so nobly advanced.

*It is rather for us to be here dedicated to the great task remaining before us – that from these honoured dead we take increased devotion to that cause for which they here gave the last full measure of devotion – that we here highly resolve that these dead shall not have died in vain – that this nation, under God, shall have a new birth of freedom – and that **government of the people, by the people, for the people, shall not perish from the Earth.***

Abe's speech **only lasted two and a half minutes**: it was so short that the official photographer didn't have time to set up his camera. When Abe was finished, the silence continued. He turned, and his footsteps creaked as he walked back across the boards towards his seat. William was sitting nearby, looking at him with a strange expression on his face.

'It's a failure,' Abe said. 'The people are disappointed.'

William raised one eyebrow . . . and winked.

That's when the applause started – just a smattering at first, then louder and louder. Abe turned again to face the crowd. They were clapping, jumping to their feet, roaring their hearts out. His speech might have been short, but it had blown his audience away.

With his carefully chosen words, Abe had given new meaning not just to the war, but to the nation's whole future. His speech did more than honour the soldiers' sacrifice. He was challenging the American people to make that sacrifice worthwhile, to finish what they'd started – **the task of building a nation dedicated to freedom and equality**.

He did get one thing wrong. Abe said that the world wouldn't remember the words he spoke that day. More than 150 years later, they are known all over the world. The Gettysburg Address is quite possibly the most famous speech ever made.

> Not bad, considering I dashed it off the night before!

Abe Dodges A Bullet

So, had it done the trick? Did the speech unite the people to push on through to victory? Well, in the summer of 1864, Abe was about to find out for certain. It was four years since he'd won the presidency, and that meant it was **time for another election**.

Now he had to begin campaigning all over again, and he started with a bang: he promised that if he was elected, he'd change the Constitution, the highest law in the land, to ban slavery throughout the United States – for ever. His Proclamation had only freed the slaves in the rebel states, and Abe had always worried that it might be overturned once the rebellion was over. But if the people voted for Abe's new promise, and the Constitution was changed, no one could ever undo it.

Abe made his position very clear, but with the rebels still fighting bravely and Union soldiers dying by the thousand, this wasn't a great time for him to be fighting an election – which was good news for the Democrats. They were saying black people deserved to be slaves, and certainly didn't deserve to have white soldiers dying to free them. They blamed the war on Abe: if he hadn't been so stubborn about slavery, the rebels would have made peace by now. It was a horrible, racist campaign designed to whip up **anger and hatred** – and it was working.

Abe was now in danger of losing much more than his presidency . . .

August 1864 – The Road Out Of Washington

It was late, and Abe was going for a ride alone. Usually he'd be escorted by armed guards, but tonight he'd managed to give them the slip. Now he was ambling along, with nothing but the sounds of the night all around him. With his presidential campaign hanging in the balance, Abe was so deep in thought, he didn't notice something stirring in the bushes off to the side of the road.

A shot rang out, and before Abe knew it, his hat was flying off his head and his horse was bolting at full gallop.

Whoa!

Abe never found out who had tried to kill him that night. He even joked about it...

> All I'd lost was my hat!

...but the hatred that made the unknown assassin pull the trigger was deadly serious. Everyone was sick and tired of the war. Ulysses S. Grant was gradually grinding down Robert E. Lee's army, but it was slow and bloody work. William Sherman hadn't been heard from in weeks. The future looked uncertain, the Democrats were blaming everything on Abe, and even his friends were telling him **he was going to lose the election**.

But in a sudden twist of fortune, on 2nd September 1864, Abe finally got the news he needed. William Sherman had captured Atlanta – the capital of Georgia, and a key supply station for the rebel armies. The Southern Confederacy was split in two. **Overnight, everything changed**.

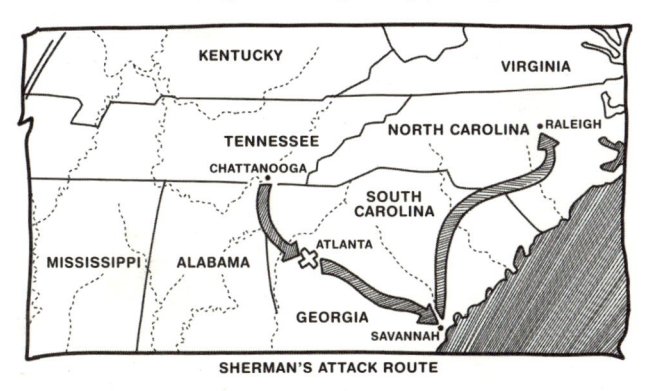

SHERMAN'S ATTACK ROUTE

Now they had a victory, people who'd been angry at Abe the day before were suddenly waving flags and singing his praises. The tide had turned again, and the people were hailing Abe as a hero.

An End In Sight

Abe won the 1864 election by a landslide. Straight away – even before he was sworn into office – he made good his promise and changed the Constitution. From now on, slavery would never again be allowed to exist in the United States.

Thousands lined the streets on 4th March 1865, for Abe's second swearing-in as president. **Half of those people were black – and free**. When he'd first come to Washington, Abe had seen people just like them chained in the streets as slaves. Now, thanks to the change he had made, they were there of their own free will.

In his speech that day, Abe talked about the war. It was more terrible than anyone could have imagined, he said; but even so, it could not match the blood and suffering of 250 years of slavery. Maybe the war was God's punishment. Maybe peace would only come when the debt of slavery was repaid in full.

Frederick Douglass was among the thousands of black people listening to Abe's speech. He was overjoyed to hear such brave words. But not everyone agreed.

In a different part of the crowd, an actor named John Wilkes Booth was listening to the very same words, with very different emotions.

Maybe it was because he'd never had the courage to actually fight for his beliefs (he'd promised his mother not to); maybe it was because he wasn't a very good actor (his brother Edwin was much more famous than him); but John Wilkes Booth had a lot of rage in his heart, and he couldn't stand the idea of black people being equal to him.

For months now he'd been communicating with **rebel spies**. Lately, he'd been mulling over a plot to strike at the president himself. Abe's speech that day made him more determined than ever.

10   Abe's Happiest Day

On 14th April 1865, Abe woke up smiling. The war was finally coming to an end: Ulysses S. Grant had captured Richmond, and just a few days earlier, General Lee had surrendered. Now Abe could start thinking about the future beyond the war. Somehow, Abe had to find a way for North and South, black and white, to live together in peace.

In the morning, he met with his ministers and made plans for rebuilding the South. After eating an apple for lunch, he signed a pardon for a young man who'd been spying for the rebels – he was more useful to Abe if he was alive than if he was dead.

That afternoon, Abe went for a carriage ride in the countryside with Mary. They discussed what they might do after Abe's second term as president was over. Maybe they'd have a chance to travel? They'd head out to the Rocky Mountains and California, sail across to Europe and maybe even Asia . . . then come back home to Illinois, to their comfortable house and Abe's familiar, messy old law office. It was years since they'd felt so cheerful.

After an early supper with friends, Abe and Mary drove out again to the theatre. **Abe gave his bodyguard the night off**. What could possibly go wrong?

A Silly Comedy

All through the war, Abe had carried on going to the theatre. He especially liked comedies: they helped take his mind off things.

> And, oh boy, I'd needed that!

The play that night was a British comedy called *Our American Cousin* – the perfect show to round off a perfect day. The first act had already started when Abe and Mary arrived, but the actors stopped mid-sentence when they saw them come in. The audience rose to their feet, **clapping and cheering**. The band played 'Hail to the Chief'. Abe smiled, bowed and sat down beside Mary in the presidential box.

Mary snuggled up beside him, resting her hand on his knee. Abe settled back to watch the play, at peace with the world. The war was over. The future lay ahead of them, and it was looking good.

Abe had quite a silly sense of humour, and his laugh was famously loud: one friend said it sounded like the neighing of a wild pony. He was soon guffawing at the jokes in the play, so it's quite possible he never heard the door of the presidential box opening, or the footsteps coming up behind him.

John Wilkes Booth cocked his pistol, pointed it at the back of Abe's head, and fired.

It was twelve minutes past ten, on the night of Good Friday.

'THEY HAVE SHOT THE PRESIDENT!'

When the gunshot rang out and they saw a man leap from the presidential box down onto the stage, most of the audience thought it was just part of the play.

Then came the screams. Mary was leaning out over the edge of the box, her eyes frantic. 'They have shot the president!' she shrieked. 'They have shot the president!'

Abe had taken a bullet to the back of the head. It would have killed most men instantly, but **Abe was so big and strong** that he was still alive when they carried him to a house across the street. He was still alive when they summoned a doctor to try to save him. But as soon as the doctor saw the bullet wound in the base of his skull, he shook his head. **No one could survive this**, not even the president.

Abe lasted nine hours. He never regained consciousness. The last thing he knew was Mary's hand in his, her warmth as she snuggled up to him, and his own hearty laughter at a silly British joke.

At 7.22, on the morning of 15th April 1865, he died.

The Plot

The president wasn't the only target that night. John Wilkes Booth had gathered together a group of men determined to stop Abe in his tracks, and just to be sure no one carried on his mission after he was dead, they planned on killing others too.

While the Lincolns were enjoying the theatre, another assassin was rampaging through William Seward's house, stabbing and clubbing at everyone who got in his way. William's sons and his bodyguard were badly hurt. William himself was very nearly killed. When the doctor arrived and saw all the carnage, he couldn't believe it was the work of just one man.

Luckily, the doctor managed to save them all, though William's face was scarred for life.

IMMORTAL ABE

William Seward got up from his bed two days later, on Easter Sunday. He was still weak, and his family hadn't told him about Abe – they were worried **the shock might kill him**. But as William looked out of the window and saw the War Department flag had been lowered in mourning . . . he knew. In any case, Abe was his friend, and William was at death's door. Abe would have come to see him by now.

'The president is dead,' he said. He lay back down on the bed, tears streaming down his face. His beloved chief, the man who'd first defeated him then joined him in the fight against slavery, was gone.

In Rochester, New York, Frederick Douglass could

hardly believe the news. He was sitting at the back of the crowded city hall as leading citizens paid tribute to Abraham Lincoln. His president. His friend.

The last speaker had finished, but people weren't leaving. Someone was tugging at Frederick's sleeve saying, 'They want you.'

Frederick walked up to the platform **with no speech prepared**. Instead, he used the words he'd heard Abe speak just five months before, after winning the presidency for the second time, about the horror of the civil war being the price to be paid for 250 years of slavery. No one could have guessed that Abe would end up paying with his own life so soon afterwards . . .

At the end, Frederick added:

Those memorable words . . . will live immortal in history.

Well – that was definitely true: **you can still read Abe's words today**, and as long as there are history books, you can be sure Abe's words will be in them.

ABE FOR EVERYONE!

If you think Abe's life story is inspiring, you're in very good company . . .

Leo Tolstoy
One of the greatest writers of all time.

Lincoln was a hero for all mankind!

Franklin D. Roosevelt
The president who helped millions of Americans out of poverty . . . then led his country to victory in the Second World War.

He fought his fight to the end.

Martin Luther King
The man who led the struggle for black people's rights 100 years after Abe's death; gave his most famous speech on the steps of the Lincoln Memorial in Washington.

He gave a beacon of light to millions of slaves.

150 years after Abe's death, America got its first black president. And guess who inspired him . . .

Barack Obama

He made my story possible.

Stop, stop: I'm blushing!

Funnily enough, although he always wanted to do great things, Abe never took himself too seriously. He laughed about people trying to kill him! But he was always serious about his mission in life: from a childhood of violence and poverty, he went all the way to the White House . . . and then battled his way through **the toughest times any US president has ever had to face**.

Abe's brilliant speeches convinced people that liberty and equality were worth fighting for – not just in his own time, but ever since. If you live in a country where those ideals are still around today – well, it's more than likely you've got Abe Lincoln to thank for it.

And if you've ever dreamed of changing the world, and wondered if that was possible for someone like you . . . ?

Just remember where I started out!

Timeline

I could have done so much more.

1809   12th February – Abraham Lincoln is born in a cabin in Kentucky, USA.

1816   The Lincoln family move to Indiana to start a new life.

1818   Abe's ma dies.

1822   Abe has to leave school aged 13 to earn money – he's had just one year of schooling.

1826   Abe goes to trial for ferrying passengers without a licence – and wins!

1828   April – Abe sets off on a trading trip to New Orleans and witnesses slavery first hand.

1830   The Lincolns move again, this time to Illinois.
Abe finally leaves home when he gets a job at a store in New Salem.
He takes part in his first election – and loses.

1834   Abe is elected to the Illinois General Assembly and his political career really begins.

1835   Abe's business partner dies and he is left to settle the debts.

1837   Abe moves to Springfield and becomes a junior partner in his friend's law firm.

1838   Abe makes the final speech at his first murder trial – and wins.

1842   Abe and Mary Todd announce their intention to marry . . . and promptly hold a ceremony that same day!

1843   Abe becomes a dad when Mary gives birth to a son, Robert.

1846   Abe is elected to Congress.
A second son, Eddie, is born.

1848   Abe campaigns for Zachary Taylor, helping him to become US president.
He meets the amazing William Seward.

1850   Eddie dies, aged three.
Another son, Willie, is born.

1853   Mary gives birth to a fourth son, Thomas (Tad).

1854   Abe starts campaigning against slavery.

1858   Abe loses the election for the Senate to his rival Stephen Douglas.
The *Illinois Gazette* tips Abe to be the next president.

1860   Abe becomes the Republican presidential candidate.
He wins the election and really will become next the US president!

1861 4th March – Abe's first day in office.
April – the American Civil War begins.

1862 Willie Lincoln dies, aged 11.

1863 Abe signs the Emancipation Proclamation, freeing slaves in the rebel states.
He gives the Gettysburg Address.

1864 Abe survives an attempt on his life.
William Sherman captures Atlanta – a long-needed victory for the Union.
Abe wins the election for his second term in office by a landslide.

1865 The House of Representatives pass the 13th Amendment, banning slavery.
Abe is sworn in for his second term as president.
The civil war ends.
Abe is shot by John Wilkes Booth and dies the next day.

2009 Barack Obama becomes America's first black president,
144 years to the month after the 13th Amendment was passed.

Glossary

abolish
To put an end to something.

abolitionist
Someone who wants to stop slavery.

address
A speech given to a large audience.

artillery
Guns that are too large to carry, sometimes mounted on wheels, like cannons.

assassinate
To murder an important person.

assembly
see General Assembly

battle tourism
Travel to current or past war zones, for sightseeing or study.

beacon
A bright light that signals a warning or is used for guidance.

bewildered
To be confused.

bluff, to call someone's
When someone attempts to deceive another that they can or will do something.

candidate
A person who is nominated for or is trying to win an election.

cargo
Goods carried by a vehicle such as a ship or aircraft.

carnage
Killing on a huge scale.

compromise
When two sides both make sacrifices to reach an agreement.

conceive
To think up a plan.

confederate
A soldier or citizen of the Southern rebel states.

confounded
Confused, mixed up.

Congress
This law-making body ran the 26 states of America. It was made up of the Senate and the House of Representatives.

congressional
Something related to Congress, e.g. congressional election.

consecrate
To declare something holy.

convention
A big formal meeting where like-minded people gather to make decisions.

dapper
Neat and stylish in appearance and dress.

dedicate
To formally devote a thing or place to the memory of someone.

delegate
Somebody chosen to speak or act for others.

Democrat
US party that, in the 19th century, represented working men and slave-owners.

devious
Someone or something that is cunning or dishonest.

devotion
Love or loyalty for a person or thing.

dither
To delay or put off making decisions.

emancipation
The freeing of people from slavery.

equality
Having equal rights, status and opportunities.

federal
Concerning the government of the whole country, not individual regions.

flabbergasted
Completely shocked or amazed!

gallery
An indoor balcony where spectators can watch what's happening in a court of law.

garrison
A group of troops defending a fort or town.

general assembly
Local government in each US state.

graduate
To successfully complete a school or college course.

hallow
To make something holy.

homestead
A family home and connected land, e.g. a farmhouse.

House of Representatives
The 'lower house' of Congress, directly elected by voters across the whole of the United States.

hunch
A feeling that something in particular is going to happen.

144

hypocrite
Someone who acts in a way that is different from what they say they believe.

illiterate
Unable to read or write.

immortal
Something or someone that never dies.

inconsolable
When someone's grief cannot be comforted.

jury
A group of members of the public who listen to a legal case and look at evidence to decide whether the person accused is guilty.

landslide
When one side in an election wins by a huge number of votes.

land surveyor
Somebody who measures and maps areas of land.

liberty
Freedom.

lobby
A group of people who try to persuade law-makers to vote in a particular way.

majority
For a political party to win an election they need to win the 'majority' of the votes (i.e. the most votes).

mill
Industrial building where materials like flour or sugar are processed.

nominate
To put a candidate forward for election.

optimistic
To be confident that things will turn out well.

plantation
A large area of land used to grow sugar, cotton or other crops.

pomp
A splendid display.

Potawatomi
A tribe of North American Indians whose name means 'people of the place of fire'.

prairie
A very large area of fertile, grassy land.

railway depot
A large railway station where trains are stored and repaired.

rampage
To move about furiously or wildly.

rebel
Someone who fights against their own government, e.g. members of the Southern Confederate army.

rebellion
Armed resistance against the lawful government or leader.

recruit
A person who joins the armed forces; to encourage someone to join the armed forces.

Republican
In the 19th century, a party formed to fight the spread of slavery.

saddlebags
Bags hanging from a horse saddle to store food, clothing and equipment.

Senate
The 'upper house' of the US Congress, elected by politicians from the 26 states.

senator
A member of the Senate. The Senate had fewer members than the House of Representatives, and senators were considered more important.

squalor
A filthy and wretched condition, usually as a result of living in neglect or poverty.

State Capitol
The building where the government of a state have their meetings.

steamer
A huge ship propelled by steam engines.

strategy (military)
The overall plan or direction of a war.

telegraph
A system that sends messages along wires using coded electrical impulses – like a very early text message!

term
The period of time a president spends in office before an election has to be called. A presidential term in the US is four years.

territory
An area of land that is connected to a particular government or ruler.

treason
A crime that involves betraying your country.

Union
The United States as a single, undivided country. During the American Civil War it came to mean the group of Northern free states that were loyal to Abe (Union soldiers were also known as Yankees).

unwarrantably
When something is done without justification.

Whig
An early US political party that stood for progress, big business and industry.

Yankees
See Union

INDEX

Use these pages for a quick reference!

A

abolitionists 67, 73–4
American Civil War 97–132, 139
anti-war speeches 65, 81
Antietam, Battle of 116, 119
Armstrong, Jack 36–7, 41, 53
assassination plots 96, 130–1, 133, 135–8
Atlanta, Battle of 131

B

birth 7
Black Hawk 41–2, 44
black soldiers 120–1, 124–5
books
    Abe's love of 16–17, 18–19, 47, 60
    about Abe 9
Booth, John Wilkes 133, 136, 137
Border States 98, 112–13
Boston 68
British Empire 72
Brown, John 85–6

C

campaign style 43–4
Capitol Building 64
childhood 7–8, 10–19
civil rights movement 140
Clary's Grove Boys 36, 41
Confederate States/Army 98, 107, 115–17, 121, 123–4, 129, 131, 134
Congress 55, 56–7, 63, 72, 73, 75
Constitution 129
cotton 28, 30

D

death, Abe's 137
debts 47, 48, 52, 59
Democrats 39, 44, 46, 50, 68, 76, 82–3, 90, 93–4, 95, 131
Dill brothers 21–3
Douglas, Stephen 50, 52–4, 58, 60, 76, 77, 79, 80–4, 90, 93
Douglass, Frederick 110–12, 115, 117, 121, 132–3, 138–9

E

education 7, 17, 18–19, 47–8
elections 38, 57
    Abe's campaign style 43–4
    Congressional 63
    General Assembly 40, 42–4, 58, 83
    Presidential 84, 91, 94, 129–30, 131, 132
    Senate 79–84
    Everett, Edward 126

F

farm labour 19, 20
ferry, Ohio River 20–3
flatboat 8, 25–6, 31, 32
Ford's Theatre 9
Fort Sumter 97

G

General Assembly (Illinois) 38, 45, 46, 47, 49, 50, 63, 83
Gentry, Allen 25–7, 31, 32
Gentry, James 25

Gettysburg, Battle of 123–4, 126
Gettysburg Address 125–8, 129
government, structure of 56–7
Grant, Ulysses S. 121, 122–3, 131, 134
grapevine 120
Green, Bowling 37, 38, 48
grocery clerk 36–7
grocery store 42, 47

H

House of Representatives 57

I

Illinois 36, 38, 40–1, 44–5, 65–6, 76, 78–9, 81
Indiana 8, 10, 11, 12, 13, 23

K

Kansas 77, 91
Kentucky 7, 14, 23
King, Martin Luther 140

L

law 23–4, 47–8, 49–55, 58–9
Lee, Robert E. 100, 107, 115, 116, 117, 122, 123, 124, 131, 134
legacy 139, 140–1
Library of Congress 64
Lincoln, Eddie (son) 62, 75
Lincoln, Mary Todd (wife) 61–2, 75, 76, 85, 91, 104, 105, 106, 118, 125, 134, 135, 136, 137
Lincoln, Nancy (mother) 7, 10, 13–14
Lincoln, Robert (son) 62, 75, 87, 104
Lincoln, Sarah (sister) 10, 14, 15, 17, 20, 25
Lincoln, Sarah Bush (stepmother) 17–18, 20

Lincoln, Thomas (father) 7–8, 10, 11, 12–13, 14–16, 17, 19, 35, 36, 53
Lincoln, Thomas ('Tad') (son) 76, 102, 104, 106, 125
Lincoln, Willie (son) 76, 104, 105–6
log cabins 7, 11, 17
Louisiana 27

M

McClellan, George B. 107, 115, 116, 117, 122
Manassas, Battles of 102, 115
marriage 61–2
Mexican War 64–6, 68, 114
milk sickness 13
Mississippi River 26–7, 31–3, 34, 121–2
murder trial 52–4, 59

N

Native Americans 41
Nebraska 77
New Orleans 25, 31, 33–5
nickname 48

O

Obama, Barack 140
Offutt, Denton 36
Ohio River 11, 21, 25–6

P

Pate, Samuel 22–3
peacemaker 75–6
plantations 27, 30, 31, 34
politics 38–40, 55, 61
    Abe enters 44–6
    see also elections; presidency
Polk, James 64–5, 72

presidency 56
  Abe holds 96–137
  Abe's campaign for 84–95
Proclamation 113–14, 117–19, 129

R

railways 21, 39, 100
Republican National Convention 88–9
Republicans 78–9, 82–3, 85, 86, 90, 92
Richmond, Battle of 115
river journey 25–7, 31–5
Roosevelt, Franklin 140

S

Sangamon County 40, 42, 44, 46
Sauk tribe 41
Senate 56, 84
Seward, William 68–71, 85, 86, 87, 88–9, 90, 92, 93, 114, 119, 125, 128, 137–8
Sherman, William 122–3, 131
shooting animals 12
slavery 8, 27–30, 32, 33–5, 39, 40
  campaign against 46, 68–74, 77–84, 112–14, 117–19, 124–5
  freeing slaves 120–1, 129, 132–3
  North-South divide 66–8, 72, 76–7, 85, 93, 95, 96, 97, 98–9, 134
  slave markets 35, 63, 71
  slave ships 28–9
  slave-owners 72–4, 93
  see also American Civil War; Proclamation
South Carolina 95, 97
Sparrow, Dennis (cousin) 7, 13, 14, 20
Sparrow, Elizabeth 13
Sparrow, Thomas 13
Speed, Joshua F. 49, 50, 60
Springfield 46, 47, 49, 50, 59, 63, 75, 82, 95
State Assembly 57
storytelling 19, 24–5, 37
Stuart, John 44, 45–6, 47, 49, 51–2, 54, 55, 58
sugar plantations 27, 30, 31

T

tanks 123
Taylor, Zachary 68, 70, 71
telegraph 100, 120
tobacco 28, 30
Todd, Mary *see* Lincoln, Mary Todd
Tolstoy, Leo 140
trials 22–4, 47, 51–4
Truett, Henry 52–4

U

Union States/Army 99, 100–3, 106–7, 114–17, 121, 122–4, 129, 131, 134

V

Vandalia 44–5
Vicksburg, Battle of 121–2
voting rights 57, 61

W

Washington DC 39, 55, 58, 63–4, 71–2, 96, 100–1, 103
weapons 100
Whigs 38–9, 44, 61, 68, 70, 78
wrestling 8, 31, 32, 36–7

Y

Yankees *see* Union states

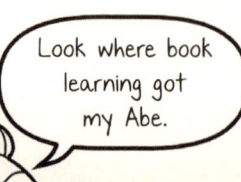

Here's a sneak preview of first names:

Emmeline
PANKHURST

first names

Emmeline PANKHURST

Haydn Kaye

Illustrations by Michael Cotton-Russell

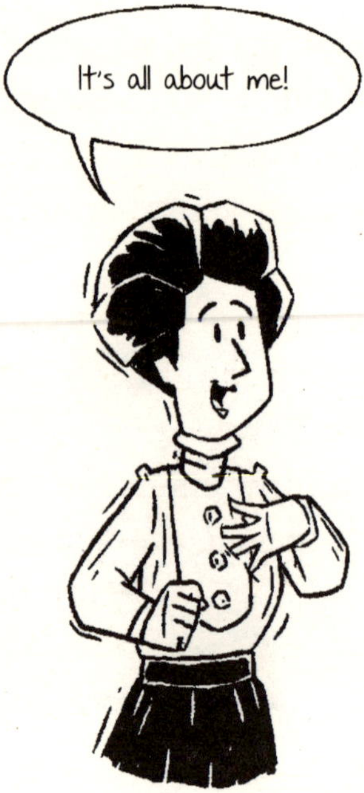
It's all about me!

Introduction – Emmeline Hears Something Strange

THE PLACE: A big family house just outside the city of Manchester, England.
THE TIME: Around the year 1870.

Emmeline couldn't get to sleep. She didn't know why, she just couldn't. Hours seemed to pass and still she lay awake. Finally she heard the stairs creak. Now it had to be *really* late – her mum and dad were coming to bed.

But Emmeline's parents didn't go straight to their room. Instead they went to check on all their other children and cooed sweet nothings over each little snoring bundle in turn. Emmeline had nine brothers and sisters, so this seemed to go on for hours.

Emmeline began to wonder: What would they say about *me* if I was asleep? Something glowing, surely. I'm such a helpful girl, and people are always saying how good I am at things. At last she heard her parents tiptoeing up to her bedside.

Suddenly she had an idea. She shut her eyes tight, breathed slowly and steadily, and pretended to be out for the count. Then she lay still and waited for the heaps of praise to come her way. **And she waited. And waited...**

Something was wrong. Why were her parents just standing there saying nothing? Emmeline's heart thumped. Had she done something to upset them? What was it? Her dad sighed and turned to go. And only then, as he stepped out of the room, did he say in the softest, saddest voice to Emmeline's mum:

What a pity she wasn't born a lad.

What on earth do you mean? Emmeline wanted to shout after him. Are boys supposed to be better than girls or something!

But she didn't shout. She couldn't. She was too puzzled by what she'd heard, and quite upset by it too. But in the days that followed she started noticing that her dad wasn't the only one who said such things. Just about everybody seemed to think men mattered more than women – and lots of wives didn't seem to mind acting like their husbands' servants either.

That felt horribly unfair to Emmeline. So when she grew up she decided to speak out about it, on behalf of women everywhere . . .

FLYING THE FLAG FOR ALL FEMALES

'Women are as good as men!' Emmeline protested loud and clear. 'Women should be men's equals, not their slaves!' And she got thrown into prison for saying it, again and again. So, in protest, **she very nearly starved herself to death**!

Newspapers all over the world reported her every move. Not just what she did herself, but what she inspired an army of her female fans to do – because in spite of hating all violence, Emmeline started a kind of war. It was a war to get women treated as men's equals so that life could be better for everyone. In a heartfelt speech at London's Albert Hall in 1912 she declared that her army was on a mission:

Although she was very small (her shoe size was just three and a half), Emmeline liked to think big. In her fight for a fair deal for women she gave everything she'd got, and never once stopped believing she would win . . .

"Now just hold your horses! I don't much like the start of this story."

I'm sorry?

"You made it sound as if my father didn't like me!"

Oh, I didn't mean . . .

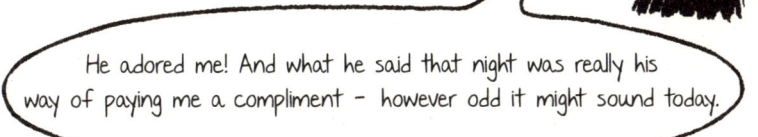

"He adored me! And what he said that night was really his way of paying me a compliment – however odd it might sound today."

I was about to explain that in the next chapter . . .

"And I didn't just protest all the time, either. You won't forget to mention that I also had the most wonderful husband, and no fewer than nine children?"

It's all going to be in here. Your family, your fame, your long fight for freedom . . .

"Oh, is it?"

The whole roller-coaster life of The Amazing Emmeline – from girl to granny, from English housewife to worldwide megastar!

"Well then, what are we waiting for? On with my story. Chop chop!"

1   Emmeline Falls Out With Her Father

Parents aren't supposed to have favourites, but everyone knew little Emmeline Goulden was her dad's. She was never any trouble, and she was good at all sorts of stuff – like being able to read before she was four years old. When she was a bit older, she would **read the morning paper to her dad** while he ate his breakfast.

There were five girls in the Goulden family. Emmeline, born in 1858, was the eldest. Growing up, she spent lots of time helping her mum to look after the other girls and her five younger brothers too. She really was the family's top child, **the Golden Goulden**.

My brothers would call me The Dictionary because I seemed to know everything!

What does antidisestablishmentarianism mean, Emmeline?

The family lived in a detached white house called Seedley Cottage. It wasn't really a cottage – it was actually much bigger and more comfortable than most other people's houses at that time. There were plenty of fields and woods nearby for the kids to have fun in, as well as the cottage's own rolling gardens, but the busy city of Manchester wasn't far away.

The world back then was massively different from now. There were no cars or bikes, so if any of the Gouldens wanted to travel quickly to Manchester or further away, they had to use a horse. Think of all the things you have to plug into electric sockets today. Not a single one of them had been invented in Emmeline's time.

There were no cinemas either, but there were theatres, where the Goulden children loved to watch their dad get up on stage and act in plays. Acting was just a hobby for him; his day job was running a clothes factory. He'd started out as an errand boy and worked his way up to become the boss, but he never forgot how hard life had been for him at the beginning, and like Emmeline's mum he did whatever he could to help other people who were still struggling.

Emmeline was proud of her dad's achievements, and he was proud of hers. On top of that, **they loved each other to bits**.

But however much they really love each other, dads and daughters don't always see eye to eye over everything . . .

The Truth Dawns On Emmeline

Even a girl as clever as Emmeline had to go to school. She was, of course, near the top of her class. But she'd always noticed something odd about what happened at school, and after a while it began to annoy her. The boys had lessons like we have today, but she and the other girls were forever being given tips on how to be 'ladylike' – how to make the home nice for their male relations by dusting furniture, arranging flowers, and that kind of thing.

This puzzled Emmeline because no one taught her brothers how to make the house look nice for their sisters. It didn't seem fair.

Something else puzzled and irritated her too. There was no end of talk about all her brothers' job prospects. One was going to help their dad to run the factory, another would be a painter, another an actor . . . **No one ever spoke about what the Goulden girls might do when they grew up**. For a while Emmeline really couldn't work out what was going on. Then at last she got it:

> Oh, right! People really do think boys are better than girls!

To finish the story, see first names: **Emmeline** Pankhurst ISBN: 978-1-910989-61-6